Second Edition

Reading the Bible
A Guide

E. H. Rece
Emory University

William A. Beardslee
Emory University

96
Prentice-Hall, Inc., *Englewood Cliffs, New Jersey*

For Marie and Kit

PRENTICE-HALL INTERNATIONAL, INC., *London*
PRENTICE-HALL OF AUSTRALIA, PTY., LTD., *Sydney*
PRENTICE-HALL OF CANADA, LTD., *Toronto*
PRENTICE-HALL OF INDIA PRIVATE LIMITED, *New Delhi*
PRENTICE-HALL OF JAPAN, INC., *Tokyo*
PRENTICE-HALL DE MEXICO, S.A., *Mexico City*

Third printing ...... June, 1965

Library of Congress Catalog Card Number: 64-10253

Printed in the United States of America
[C]

Preface

This book is designed to make possible an intelligent discussion of the meaning of the Bible. It emphasizes reading the biblical books themselves and contains questions to stimulate thought about the meaning of *what* is read as well as to focus attention on pertinent facts.

Certain parts of the Bible have been selected for careful study. Major emphasis in the Old Testament is placed on the history, the prophets, and the Wisdom Literature; in the New Testament on the synoptic gospels, Paul and John. Briefer guides are provided for the remaining books, ranging from reading assignments and questions to brief descriptions. The Supplementary Materials, pages 171-189, provide several schematic summaries of information, including an outline of biblical history which may serve as a reference guide for relating the different parts of the Bible.

In addition to its usefulness for the individual Bible reader, this book can be used as a guide for an adult church school or community Bible study group. Both the individual reader and the group leader should stay away from lengthy discussion of isolated texts, however, and concentrate on the messages of the books as complete works.

It would be useful to have available these reference books: (1) a modern translation of the Bible—the Revised Standard Version or the Goodspeed-Smith translation; (2) a book on the approach to the Bible, such as Wright and Fuller's *The Book of the Acts of God*; (3) a book that gives at least minimum historical background, such as *The Westminster Historical Atlas to the Bible*.

Teachers using the Guide in formal courses will recognize that the suggested readings in interpretative books can be adjusted or supplemented according to the scope of the course.

Acknowledgments

We wish to acknowledge the indebtedness we owe the many scholars whose original work has made this particular book possible. Part of our debt to them will be paid if some who are introduced to the Bible through this volume are inspired to continue its study.

Certain specific acknowledgments must be made. We have followed the chronology of G. E. Wright and F. V. Filson in *The Westminster Historical Atlas to the Bible*, revised edition (Philadelphia: Westminster Press, 1956), fitting the literature into it. All quotations from the Bible are reprinted from *The Bible: An American Translation* (copyright 1948), translated by J. M. P. Smith, Edgar J. Goodspeed, and others, by permission of the University of Chicago Press. A part of the "Hymn to the Sun" is reprinted from Elmer A. Leslie's *The Psalms* (copyright 1949), by permission of the Abingdon Press (Nashville, Tenn.). The Babylonian story of the Flood is reprinted from E. A. Speiser's translation of the Gilgamesh Epic in *Ancient Near Eastern Texts Relating to the Old Testament*, edited by James B. Pritchard (copyright 1950, 1955) by permission of the Princeton University Press.

We are indebted to Mr. John S. McKenzie for drawing the maps.

During the last twenty-five years, half a dozen other men have used some or most of the material in *Reading the Bible* in conducting a course in the English Bible. Each has made his contribution toward this book. In the preparation of the second edition, we have been particularly indebted to the incisive comments of our colleague, Martin J. Buss. We wish to thank Mrs. Martha McKay for her careful work on the manuscript.

It is our hope that this book will help others to discover some of the meaning and beauty, the solace and inspiration, that abound so richly in the Bible. Even more devoutly we hope it will lead many, through the Bible, to find the God whose Word it is.

E. H. Rece

William A. Beardslee

Table of Contents

List of Maps

1

The Study of the Bible

Revelation in History

The Bible has made the history of the Hebrews and early Christianity familiar to our culture. The history it records is very ancient, but the influence of that history permeates almost every aspect of modern life—particularly our laws, literature, art, music, morals, and architecture.

While the Bible has influenced our culture, it has come down to us because it affords a foundation for religious faith. Christians and Jews alike find in the Bible a history that is unique, because it not only records the story of the lives of the ancients but also reveals the meaning of life itself. In this history God touched the lives of men, and through it He reaches men today. To bring this faith into clearer focus is much of the purpose of this book.

The Bible is not a single book, but a collection of books. It was composed and written in several languages over a period of more than a thousand years. Its most recent works are almost two thousand years old. To understand these books we need to know as much as possible about the background of the times in which they found their present form.

In one way, the men of the Bible lived in a world that was the same as ours. They were born; they lived and died. They saw the sun and the moon, knew hunger and cold, sought affection and peace, were aroused to anger and passion; they fought and loved, and they knew the deep discontent that will not let a man rest until he finds a consciousness of communion with his Creator.

Yet, in another way, the world of these men was a completely different one from ours. They lived on a "flat" earth that floated on the "waters beneath the earth" and was covered by the "heavens above the earth." They lived in a world in which slavery was a widespread condition and in which technology in any modern sense was unknown. Most important of all, for their world, God was the cause of all things: war and peace, health and plague, famine and plenty were all direct expressions of God's will. Insofar as modern man has lost his intimate sense of God's reality and power, he has paid too dearly for his increase in knowledge of, and control over, his environment.

To study the Bible historically is to confront our world with the ancient world. This does not mean simply a process of learning dates and names; it means learning to understand the life and thought of another time. Precisely because the Bible itself is so much concerned with history is it important to study it with the legitimate tools of historical scholarship. We must understand its story as a portion of the history of mankind in order better to see the meaning the men of the Bible saw in the events of their times. For them, God's confrontation with life was particularly centered in His struggle with human history.

We must remember also that we can understand ancient people only because they were human beings such as we are. As we consider the differences between their views of life and the attitudes common today, we shall find that one central theme of the Bible confronts us particularly: its view of God's work in history. We shall thus be led from the study of the historical past to a fresh inquiry into the meaning of history. The Bible sees history as present as well as past. The remembered mighty works of God revealed the God who is creating and controlling the present. That He will determine the future is taken for granted.

New Insights from Historical Study

While the Church has been interested in questions of authorship and dates of biblical books from as early as the second century, the exact and thorough historical methods now used are a product of the past two centuries. Before that time the Bible was the only literature from the ancient world of Mesopotamia, Palestine, and Egypt known to western man. In these two centuries thousands of documents in several languages have been recovered and translated. Now we know as much of the world in which the Hebrews lived as we do of any other ancient civilization.

As these ancient documents were deciphered the scholars were faced with the problems of: who wrote them, when they were written, and where and for what purpose they were written. As they began to answer these questions, the study of these documents influenced Bible study at two points: biblical times took on a third dimension as we came to have a picture of the parallel history of the Hebrews' neighbors; and the methods of historical study that had proved so valuable when applied to ancient Assyrian, Babylonian, and Egyptian documents proved equally rewarding as a method of studying the ancient Hebrew and Christian documents.

Such study has been of great value. It has indicated how the tremendous changes that take place over a long period of time help explain the differences between the primitive songs of Lamech, Miriam, and Deborah, on the one hand, and the great sermons of the prophets and Jesus on the other. Contradictions between the accounts or messages of different books are understood when these books are read in the context of the times out of which they came. The wonder and reverence that great passages have always elicited are doubled when the texts are placed against the background of the actual historical situations in which they were written. New meanings arise from an understanding of the meanings the passages had for the authors.

True, any new insight disturbs old patterns of thought. Because of this the new methods of study were suspect by many devout people for years. Historical study has shown, for instance, that the tradition that Moses wrote the book of Exodus is inaccurate—and old traditions die hard. Furthermore, historical study will not sustain the once popular Protestant view that the Bible is without error.

Questions of authorship or inerrancy are not, however, the basic questions. The real trouble centers in the fear that the frankly questioning approach of historical study may undermine the authority of the Bible. For both Christianity and Judaism the Bible has stood in a position of special authority. Any threat to this authority immediately raises misgivings.

Actually the authority of Scripture, in the central tradition of the church, has not rested on the *description* of the event but on the *event*. There has always been a consciousness of a difference between revelation and the *record* of the revelation. The Bible has been considered the definitive record of a story in which God acted—but the *record* only. God revealed Himself in historical events to men who responded in faith. As best they could, the authors of the Bible recorded these events and their meanings. Great poetry and epic prose give us an inspiring record, but the final authority still rests in the proclamation of God's actions in history.

Viewpoints in Confronting the Bible

The historical approach is not the only way of reading the Bible, and in fact it stands always in a certain tension with that use and understanding of the Bible which stems directly from faith. For historical study inevitably emphasizes the human element: It is by human understanding that we approach any matter historically. If we think as historians, the forces of history that we can understand are human and natural forces: the influence of climate or geography, the force of tradition, the strength or weakness of leadership, the influence of the "great man," etc. Since the Bible is, in its historical sections, one of the great sources of our modern historical thinking, it is not surprising that we find these human factors sometimes emphasized in the biblical books. But in spite of this common element, the Bible's history is, in all its variety, differently oriented. It is above all a book of worship. Its memories and stories were gathered and celebrated in festival and cult and are shaped to point to the greatness and goodness of God, who acted in the remembered events. Our "historical" thinking makes us ask exactly what happened. Their "historical" thinking made them remember and celebrate, in the context of worship, the crucial moments in which God con-

fronted them. Thus as we study the Bible we find that our primary
task is not so much understanding the bare events as it is understanding the faith and purpose of the writings that celebrate those
events. Once understood, this faith, which saw true history as the
story of the mighty acts of God, confronts the faith of the student
and affords a ground for fruitful discussion among men of varying
faiths.

The Christian sees in the Old Testament story of the calling of
a people by the righteous and holy God the preparation for the coming of Christ—the climactic event in history. The New Testament
tells how God, acting in Christ, effectively overcame the power of
sin and made His goodness not only known, but also a transform-
ing power in human life. Those whom God in Christ made new men
have left us their witness to his power in the New Testament. Thus
Christ is the ultimate revelation. In him we find the standard by
which to judge the Old Testament and also the key to the right understanding of his interpreters in the New Testament.

Readings

Read one of the following:

Anderson, *Understanding the Old Testament,* Introd. & Chap. 1.

Dodd, *The Bible Today.* Chap. 1-2.

Gottwald, *A Light to the Nations,* Chap. 1-2.

The Interpreter's Bible, Vol. I, pp. 165-71.

Wright and Fuller, *The Book of the Acts of God,* pp. 3-43.

2

Translation into English

To most English-speaking Protestants "The Bible" means the King James, or "Authorized" Version, of the English Bible. This translation is an English classic. It has influenced the language profoundly and has been the principal English version of the Bible for more than three centuries. But it is only one of several English Bibles.

For Roman Catholics the Bible contains fourteen books or portions of books not found in the King James. The English of the Douay Bible, the translation commonly used by the Roman Church, is somewhat different from that of the King James translation. Judaism's Scriptures are limited to those books found in the Old Testament. Their English translation differs from both of the Christian Bibles.

"The English Bible" is a blanket term, like "the Christian Church." No one volume can be called "the English Bible." All versions of the Bible in English are translations. The Old Testament was written in Hebrew, with the exception of a few Aramaic sections. The New Testament was written in Greek. But long before the Christian era the Old Testament had been translated into Greek and this Greek version, called the Septuagint, became the Scripture of the largest part of the early Christian church.

As the western church became more and more centered in Rome, the Scriptures were translated into a number of Latin versions. Near the beginning of the fifth century, Jerome made the accepted Latin translation from Hebrew and Greek sources. This is known as the Vulgate—the translation of the Bible into spoken Latin. It was *the* Bible of Western Europe for a thousand years.

When the Anglo-Saxons invaded the British Isles in the fifth century, they found Christianity already established there. They suppressed it ruthlessly, but a century later their kings and nobles were looking favorably on the missionary efforts of Rome. Christianity came back to the upper classes and monasteries were established. But the common people had been forgotten.

Legend tells of the vision of Caedmon, a lay brother in a seventh century monastery. Hiding the chagrin he felt because he could not sing, he was tending cattle in the stable, where he could not hear the songs of the brothers. Suddenly an angel appeared and commanded him to sing. From that night Caedmon sang. By day the learned monks told him the stories hidden in the Latin tongue of Holy Script. By night he shaped the stories into Anglo-Saxon verse. Thus minstrelsy brought the Bible and Christianity back to the serfs and shepherds of Britain.

Seven centuries later Purvey wrote: "Bede translatide the bible, and expounide myche in Saxon, that was English . . . in his tyme." But some of Caedmon's paraphrases are the earliest Anglo-Saxon versions of biblical stories now extant. The Venerable Bede was a great scholar, but his works as we know them do not include a translation of the Bible. Aelfric translated at least parts of the Bible into Anglo-Saxon toward the end of the tenth century. But the Vulgate was the Bible in England, as in the rest of Europe, until after the Renaissance.

By the middle of the fourteenth century the English language was fast growing out of its "early English" childhood, and the yeast of the Renaissance had leavened all realms of European life. John de Wycliffe undertook the task of giving the Bible to those who knew English but not Latin. Aided by Nicholay de Hereford and possibly others, he completed a translation of the Vulgate by 1382. It was almost immediately revised by John Purvey and "other good fellows" who completed their work in 1388, four years after Wycliffe's death.

Many of these men were persecuted for throwing the Gospel pearls before swine. Some were executed. In 1408 the Church forbade the reading of Wycliffe's version or any similar one and decreed "that no one shall in future translate on his own authority any text of holy scripture into the English tongue . . . by book, booklet, or treatise."

But the fifteenth century brought with it the printing press. Men's minds were quickened and communication was facilitated. More and more men sought knowledge—and the knowledge they prized most was in the Bible. In 1455 the Gutenberg Bible was printed. It was the Latin text, but it is significant that the first printed book in Europe was the Bible.

William Tyndale began his work early in the sixteenth century. Working for the first time with Hebrew and Greek sources instead of Latin, he began to publish his translations in 1525. Accused of heresy, he fled England in 1524, but his New Testament was printed on the continent and smuggled into England. He continued to work, always under a cloud, until his death at the stake in 1536. He published the New Testament (1525, revised 1534), the Pentateuch (1530), and Jonah (1531). He left the books from Joshua through Chronicles in the hands of his friend John Rogers as manuscripts.

A year before Tyndale was burned for heresy the first complete English Bible was printed and distributed openly. It was the Coverdale Bible (1535). The coincidence of these seemingly contradictory events came from the involved tangle of English affairs. Tyndale was an active reformer and so opposed Cardinal Wolsey and Sir Thomas More in matters of doctrine. He fled England to escape from Wolsey. When the issue became one of conduct he sided with Wolsey and More in opposing Henry VIII's divorce of Catherine and marriage to Anne Boleyn. Thomas Cromwell and Thomas Cranmer, who became Archbishop of Canterbury in 1533, did not oppose Henry's divorce and remarriage. They did urge the publication of an English Bible in answer to the demand of the people (witness the smuggling in of Tyndale's New Testament) and put the task into Miles Coverdale's hands. Coverdale was a friend of Tyndale but had taken no open part in the controversies of the day. Thus 1535 saw the publication of the Coverdale Bible, the arrest of Tyndale, and the execution of Sir Thomas More. Coverdale's first edition was dedicated to the King. The two editions of 1537 carry the note "Sett forth with the Kynges most gracious license." These and the contemporary "Matthew Bible" were the first licensed versions.

Coverdale mentions five sources, identifying them as Latin and German ("Dutch"). Two Latin and two German sources can be identified. There can be no doubt that Tyndale's English translation was a fifth source. In any case, Coverdale did not work directly from Hebrew or Greek sources.

The "Matthew Bible" published in 1537 is Tyndale's in all the books Tyndale had translated. This version seems to have been published by John Rogers, using the name Thomas Matthew to avoid persecution. Richard Taverner's Bible of 1539 was also based on Tyndale, although revised more copiously than the Matthew.

Tyndale's work comes definitely to the fore in the Great Bible (1539), an ambitious work commissioned by Cromwell, supported by Cranmer, and dedicated to Henry VIII. Coverdale was in charge of the editorial work on this book, and yet Tyndale's translation is followed more closely than the Coverdale. The second edition of the Great Bible (1540) was the first authorized version.

Mary, who came to the throne in 1553, persecuted the translators and burned their books along with those of other "heretics." Many Protestants fled England at this time. Gathering at Geneva, a number of these exiles worked on their own translation of the English Bible. The Geneva Bible, a careful revision of earlier translations, was published in 1560. For the first time, the present verse arrangement and Roman type faces were used. The notes in this edition naturally reflected Protestant doctrines.

The Geneva Bible was superior to the Great Bible, but its notes did not please the authorities of the Church of England. The Bishops' Bible (1568) was therefore produced to supplant it, but failed to make any great mark. In forty-three years, seven English translations had been published.

In 1582 a translation of the Latin New Testament into English was published by Roman Catholics in Rheims, France. The Old Testament was published in Douai, France, in 1610. Published as a complete Bible in 1635, this translation is known as the Rheims-Douay, or the Douay, version.

In 1604, King James I, in answer to the petition of a conference representing both Puritans and Anglicans, appointed a company of translators. They worked for seven years and published our "King James" version in 1611. This translation rested on all previous ones and shows the strength and vigor of the language's youth, inherited from Wycliffe, as well as the skill and grace of the mature Elizabethan period, which produced the translators. In their preface, the translators say:

> . . . truly, Good Christian reader, we never thought . . . to make a new translation, nor yet to make of a bad one a good one . . . but to make a good one better, or out of many good ones one principal good one, not justly to be excepted against; that has been our endeavor, that our work.

This translation was received with some criticism but soon gained its place of eminence. For two hundred fifty years it stood alone.

But the English language continued to grow and, in the nineteenth century, the discoveries of the archeologists resulted in the possession of hitherto unknown manuscripts and an improved knowledge of Hebrew and Greek. Elizabethan English was no longer the language of the people. Scholars were no longer handicapped by a minimal knowledge of documents or languages. A movement toward new translation was natural and desirable.

Soon after the middle of the century the Church of England began to discuss revision of the King James version. In 1870 groups of revisors were appointed, and in 1885 the English Revised version was published.

American scholars had contributed their ideas to the project but found most of their suggestions omitted or placed in marginal notes. As a result, the American scholars published an American Standard version in 1901.

The English Revised version and the American Standard version were both based on the King James and sought to depart from its wording as little as possible. Both gained considerable acceptance for a time but have been largely replaced by other, more recent, translations.

Recognizing the growing fruits of research and the inevitable change of English idiom, American scholars have continued their work since 1901. In 1952 the Revised Standard version was published. It is a revision of the version of 1901, much more readable and easier to understand. In many ways it is the best version of the Bible for American readers.

A number of twentieth-century scholars, however, have not been satisfied with mere revision. They have felt the need for a modern translation, and many have attempted the task. Among these, James Moffatt's *The Holy Bible: A New Translation* (New York: Harper & Row, 1922) is noteworthy as the work of one scholar; *The Bible, An American Translation,* by J. M. Powis Smith, Edgar Goodspeed, *et al.* (Chicago: University of Chicago Press, 1948) uses the American idiom and has had wide circulation; and J. B. Phillips's *The New Testament in Modern English* (New York: The Macmillan Co., 1958), a rather free translation (virtually a paraphrase), has been quite well received.

The trend toward new translations rather than revision of the King James is reflected in the work of English scholars who have been working under the joint sponsorship of all Protestant communions in the British Isles since 1946. These churches plan to publish a completely new translation of the Bible. Their first publication, *The New English Bible: New Testament* (Oxford Univ. Press and Cambridge Univ. Press, 1961) has been widely acclaimed. Work continues on the Old Testament and the Apocrypha.

Meanwhile American Jewish scholars have been at work for some years on a new English translation of the Holy Scriptures of Judaism. The Jewish Publication Society published *The Torah* in 1962. Work on *The Prophets* and *The Writings* continues. We have not come to the end of the story of the translation of the Bible into English.

Reading

The Interpreter's Bible, Vol. I, pp. 84-105.

3

Sketch of Geography of Bible Lands

Out of the mountains that lie between the Black and Caspian Seas, the Euphrates River dashes rapidly to the southwest, headed straight for the northeast corner of the Mediterranean Sea. It seems destined to enter the Mediterranean at that point and form another Nile delta, with its rich burden of mountain soil. Within almost one hundred fifty miles of this destination it changes its course and meanders for nearly a thousand miles to the Persian Gulf. In this slow southeasterly course it parallels the Tigris River, which rises in the same mountains further to the east. These two rivers form a rich alluvial valley, well-watered, fertile when properly irrigated, and shut in by mountains to the north and east and by the great Arabian desert to the west.

Another river comes out of the mountains of east-central Africa and flows fifteen hundred miles to the Mediterranean—the great Nile—with its gift of fertility to a strip of the eastern edge of the Sahara. This fertile strip also is isolated, with the desert to the west,

the Arabian desert to the east across the Red Sea, and the mountains in the far south.

The Arabian desert nearly cuts these two valleys off from each
other, but not quite. Along the eastern coast of the Mediterranean
there is a narrow fertile strip. In the center of this eastern Mediterranean coast rise the Lebanon mountains, with some peaks only a
little short of two miles high. Flowing north from the mountains,
the Orontes River parallels the coastline for some distance before it
finally turns into the sea. South of the mountains, the streams that
do not flow directly into the sea empty into the Jordan, which is a
"dead-end" river.

The Jordan River valley is unique on the face of the earth. It is
a great crack in the earth's crust. The little Sea of Galilee, a fresh
water lake fed by the snows of Mount Hermon (a few miles to the
north and more than nine thousand feet above sea level), is itself
more than six hundred fifty feet below sea level. Scarcely seventy
miles south of this lake, the Jordan ends its windings in the Dead
Sea, almost thirteen hundred feet below sea level. This great brine
vat is another thirteen hundred feet deep.

In the Egyptian and Mesopotamian valleys arose two of the
world's earliest civilizations and five of the world's earliest empires.
Natural barriers protected both Egypt and Mesopotamia from
organized invasion—except from each other. It was strategically
important, then, to control the land-bridge that connected the two
valleys. And right on this bridge—the narrow strip of land from the
desert a few miles east of Jordan to the seacoast—the Hebrews
found the Promised Land. Barely fifty by one hundred fifty miles in
size, the land of Canaan, later called Palestine (now Israel and
Jordan), was the site of the major part of biblical history. Much of
that history reflects the important part control of the bridge played
in the game of ancient empire.

The land's northern border is just north of Mount Carmel, which
juts out into the Mediterranean. In this northern section are the
Mountains of Lebanon, where grew the great cedar forests of ancient
renown. To the east and south of Mount Carmel lies the Plain of
Esdraelon, a triangular area of considerable fertility. This plain was
used by most of the great trade routes to cross over from the Jordan
valley to the coastal plain; on this plain the warriors of the world
have fought. Control of this plain was one important link in the

control of the land-bridge. Deborah was not the first to fight here, nor was Napoleon the last.

South of the Esdraelon plain, the mountains give way to hills that gradually become lower and more arid until, southwest of the Dead Sea, they are known as the Negeb or "Parched Land." Along the coast the plain increases in width and fertility, south of Mount Carmel. Immediately south of the mountain is the Plain of Sharon, where the famous "rose of Sharon" grew. Still further south the plain came to be called the Philistine plain. Here the Philistines built a number of cities of considerable importance in the Hebrew world: Gaza, Askelon, Ashdod, Ekron, Gath. East of the central hills flows the Jordan itself, twisting back and forth in its wide, worn canyon until it is about twice as long as the straight-line distance between source and mouth. East of the river valley is a narrow strip of fertility, fading quickly into the great desert.

In this tiny spot were magnificent forests and desert wastes; fertile valleys and dry plateaus, fit only for grazing; snowcapped peaks and sunken lakes; bracing mountain air and an atmosphere weighed down with six million tons of water that evaporated each day from the surface of the Dead Sea—almost all of the extremes of climate and fertility. This was the home of the Hebrews, the "Promised Land."

Reading

Read one of the following:

Gottwald, *A Light to the Nations,* pp. 57-84.

Wright and Filson, *Westminster Atlas,* rev. ed., pp. 17-22.

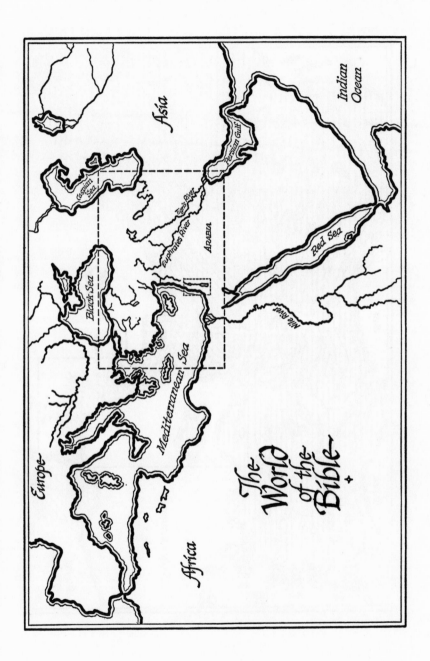

The World of the Bible

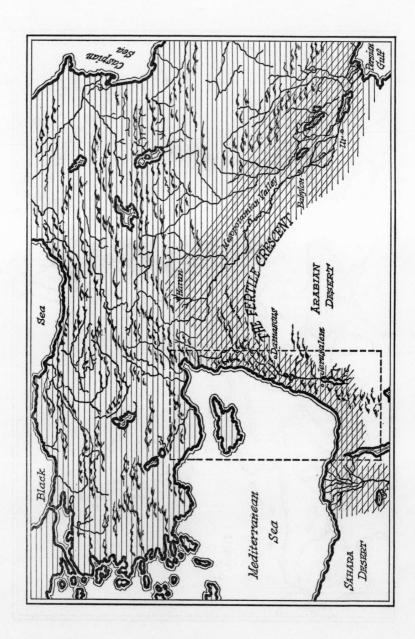

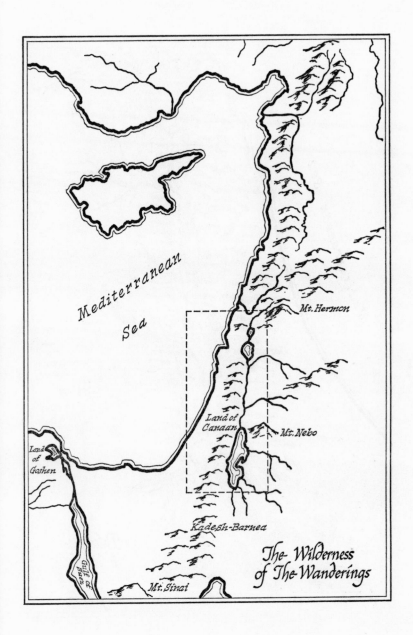

The Wilderness of The Wanderings

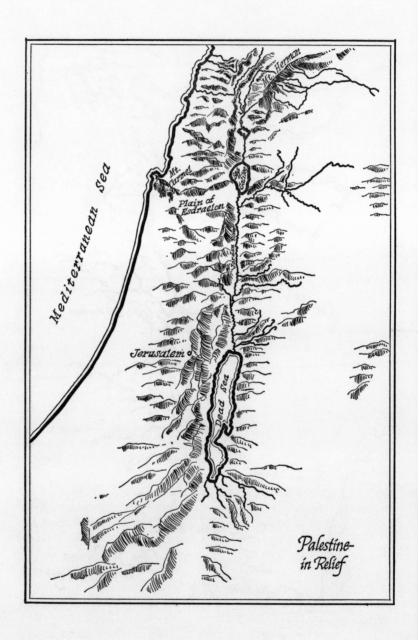

Palestine
in Relief

4

Historical Outline

The Background of Hebrew History

The history of the ancient Near East is much better known today than it was even a few decades ago, largely as a result of the studies of the remains of ancient civilizations. Before the time when men lived in cities or knew how to make metal implements, Palestine was one of the homes of Stone Age men. The growth of agriculture, the beginnings of village life, early forms of pottery, copper, and bronze work, and the growth of art and burial customs that seem to point toward religious belief—all can be seen in remains from early Palestine. The Early Bronze Age (about 3000-2000 B.C.) was the time of the first great civilizations in Egypt and Mesopotamia. In both areas large-scale irrigation projects were achieved through centralized control; farming done by the great mass of the people became the economic base for the culture, art, and, to a great extent, religion of the upper classes. This was the period during which the pyramids were built.

Among the noteworthy events of the Middle Bronze Age (about 2000-1500 B.C.) was the rule of Hammurabi

19

in Babylonia. His famous code of laws, which came before the time
of Moses, portrays the king as the protector of the weak and op-
pressed. In various details its laws parallel the Hebrew legislation,
indicating that one source of the Hebrew law was the legal tradition
of the ancient Near East. The Middle Bronze Age was the "age of
the patriarchs," when the ancestors of the Hebrews lived the life of
the wandering shepherd groups described so vividly in the book of
Genesis. Egypt was ruled by foreigners (the Hyksos) during part of
the Middle Bronze Age; it is probable that the Hebrews entered
Egypt during this period. The Late Bronze Age (about 1500-1200
B.C.), when the hated foreign rulers had been expelled from Egypt
and the oppression of the "foreign" Hebrews by the native Egyptians had begun, was the time of the Exodus from Egypt.

Palestine was under Egyptian control during most of the Middle
and Late Bronze Ages, although the Egyptians were often inefficient
and lax as rulers. Culturally, Palestine was closely attached to Syria.
The Canaanites, who lived in Palestine before the coming of the
Hebrews, had language, culture, and religion very similar to those
revealed in the newly discovered literature of Ugarit in Syria. This
literature (from about 1500 B.C.) pictures a religion in which the
wars and loves of various gods were correlated with the changing
features of nature's yearly cycle.

During the Late Bronze Age the Hebrews appear as a tribe or
nation escaping from slavery in Egypt and struggling to make a
home in Palestine. Behind them lay a considerable stay in Egypt;
before this, in turn, there had been a time of nomadic shepherd life
in southern Palestine. Of the age of the patriarchs we have only the
records of the book of Genesis to give us specific information about
the beginnings of the Hebrews. Yet archeological study has shown
that the stories of the patriarchs (Abraham, Isaac, and Jacob) reflect
the same sorts of social customs and economic life as are shown in
Middle Bronze Age remains from the Fertile Crescent. In spite of
the long stay in Egypt, the culture of the Hebrews was closer to that
of Haran and Mesopotamia than to that of the land from which
they escaped—no doubt the reason for the similarities was that the
Hebrews had moved around the Fertile Crescent into southern
Palestine, and from there to Egypt.

In all of the cultures that surrounded the Hebrews religion
played a central role, as it did in the life of the Hebrews themselves.
Naturally the Hebrews were influenced by the beliefs and practices

of their neighbors—some of their customs of sacrifice were similar to those of the Canaanites, and some of their stories of early times (especially that of the flood) are similar to those of Mesopotamia. The Hebrews were not different because they were religious, nor was their religion entirely different from the religions of their neighbors. Hebrew religion is different not in the sense that it was never influenced by other religions, but in the sense that it provided a distinctive center that gave new meaning even to practices and beliefs not uniquely their own. To the Hebrews themselves it appeared that this distinctive center of meaning was found in their encounter with God in the events of their history. Their religious thinking largely took the form of comments on their history. Therefore some knowledge of the history of the Hebrews is necessary for an understanding of the development and deepening religion of the Hebrews—a development and deepening they knew as a continuing disclosure of God in the events of their history and in the interpretation of these events by inspired men.

Old Testament Books of History

Old Testament books tell of the history of the Hebrews in two major parts and a "review." Torah ("Instruction") is the Hebrew name for the first five books (Genesis through Deuteronomy). In English these books are called The Law or the Pentateuch (five books). These books tell the story from creation to the end of the "forty years of wandering" following the exodus from Egypt. The next six books of history (Joshua through II Kings, omitting Ruth) tell the story from the entrance into the Promised Land to the exile from the land six hundred years later. The two books of Chronicles review the entire story in a later rewriting.

The book of Genesis starts with the creation and ends with Jacob (Israel) and his children in Egypt. The next four books tell of the exodus from Egypt and the forty years of wandering. Since the account of this short period is almost as long as the account of the next six hundred years and much longer than the account of all time prior to the exodus, we can assume that this was the important period in the memory of the Hebrews.

The Torah as a whole can best be understood as the interpretation and expansion in depth and detail of the affirmation of the faith found in Deuteronomy 26:5-10. Such confessions were recited as part of the act of worship on days set aside to commemorate and re-enact great events (see Deuteronomy 26:1-11). These foundation events were those that gave the community of faith its distinctive character. Their celebration in worship brought the meaning of the past into the current life of the community—put the mighty acts of God into the present tense, as it were (see Deuteronomy 5:2-3).

The history was not written just to preserve a record; nor was it written to glorify kings or other men. It was written to undergird the faith of the people in their God, who confronted not only "our forefathers" but also "those of us who are all here alive today" (Deuteronomy 5:3) with His gift of grace and His demand for obedience. The story was written to celebrate God's majesty and make the celebrants aware of His glory. It was not concerned with recording events "photographically" but with reviving their meanings, with making the celebrants immediately aware of the mystery of God's presence.

Not until long after the actual events was anything written, so that many of the details of the origin and founding of the Hebrew community must remain obscure to us. But the books give a clear picture of both the faith of the Hebrews and the fact that this faith was inextricably bound to concrete events. Only a history could record their faith.

For a fuller sketch of how the Pentateuch came to be written see pp. 82-86. Here we can note that the first great connected narrative that runs through these books—the so-called J document—was written in the tenth or ninth century B.C., three or four hundred years after the settlement of Canaan. The author aims to show that his people's settlement of the land was not by chance but was the result of God's purpose from the very beginning. Hence he gathers stories of the creation, the fall, the flood, and other stories of very early times to show how Yahweh,[1] the Hebrew God, had prepared the way for His choice of Abraham and his descendants. Then the stories of the patriarchs provide a preparation for the great

---

[1] The familiar English spelling for the name of the God of the Hebrews is Jehovah. A more accurate way to write the name is Yahweh, the form used here. The proper name of God is much more common in the Old Testament than most readers of the Bible suppose, since most of our translations follow the ancient Jewish custom of avoiding this name and referring to Yahweh as *the Lord*.

hinge-point of the story, the exodus and covenant, which is followed by the desert period and (carrying forward into the book of Joshua) the occupation of the land under God's guidance. This great narrative is now combined with others but still provides a kind of "outline" for the Pentateuch. It fills out the credal or confessional pattern that can be seen in the short statements connected with ceremonies of worship.

The J story has been combined with another, slightly later, parallel version of the story (the E document), with a priestly collection of narratives and genealogies, and with a great body of Hebrew law to make up the present Pentateuch. Much of the compiling and editing of the Pentateuch seems to have been done by priestly writers during the exile or soon thereafter. The laws include many very early elements, but they were collected and edited over a long period of time. The priestly influence is reflected in the emphasis on ceremonial purity and the Temple cult, particularly in Leviticus.

When we turn to the second group of historical books (Joshua through II Kings), we again find a variety of sources and traditions. The organizing plan of these books is supplied by the "Deuteronomistic" editors; that is, editors whose point of view reflects that of the book of Deuteronomy. They have written history so as to show how the whole story of the occupation, the judges, and the monarchy is the story of God's continually offering the people the opportunity for obedience or disobedience and how the successes and failures of the community are to be seen as the fruit of the people's choice. Simply put: when they obeyed, things went well with them; when they did not obey, they were defeated and eventually exiled. Though the Deuteronomistic history remembers moments of obedience, its over-all picture is one of the repeated failure of the people—a striking contrast to the common pattern of glorifying the nation and its leaders in a national history.

Into this framework have gone oral traditions of early times, stories of early heroes, bits of now lost early books like the book of Jashar (Joshua 10:13; II Samuel 1:18) and the book of the Wars of Yahweh (Numbers 21:14), a vivid and masterly history of much of David's and Solomon's reigns, and much information from the court records of the monarchy (I Kings 11:41; 14:29; II Kings 15:21, etc.).

These two collections of the memories of God's dealing with His people came into the Scripture separately. The Pentateuch or Law was the foundation or core of Hebrew Scripture and came to be so regarded about 400 B.C. The other historical books, the "former prophets" of the Jewish Bible, were gathered into the Scripture along with the books of the prophets perhaps about 250 B.C. For I and II Chronicles, see p. 45.

Readings

Read Deuteronomy 26 and Joshua 24 as examples of ceremonies of remembering.

Read one of the following:

Gottwald, *A Light to the Nations,* pp. 102-114.

Wright and Filson, *Westminster Atlas,* rev. ed., pp. 23-36.

Wright and Fuller, *The Book of the Acts of God,* pp. 47-135.

Outline of Hebrew History

The outline that follows divides Hebrew history into periods. Except for the last period, which is beyond the scope of the historical books in the Bible, biblical readings are listed at the end of brief statements about the period so that the reader may gain an insight into the biblical record itself.

Here, as in the following chapters, the biblical readings are the core of this book. Following the readings are questions for the reader: some intended to focus his attention on facts, some intended to stimulate discussion and thought. The reading in the Bible should be done with these questions in mind.

Experience has shown that at times instructors find it useful to shorten the readings in one or more sections. In many cases, shorter readings are listed. In all cases the longer readings include the shorter ones and are preferable. Inevitably, some questions will assume readings not found in the shortened assignment.

For a better understanding of Hebrew history, the following surveys will be useful in addition to the biblical readings and the brief supplementary readings provided for each section.

Readings

Albright, *The Biblical Period from Abraham to Ezra.*

The Interpreter's Bible, Vol. I, pp. 272-91 (*The History of Israel*).

The Interpreter's Bible, Vol. I, pp. 292-348 (*The History of the Religion of Israel*).

The Exodus and Wanderings

about 1300-1200 B.C.

about 1300   Escape from Egypt
about 1250   Hebrew invasion of Palestine

The towering figure in the story of the exodus is Moses. Though familiar with Egyptian ways, he chose to side with the enslaved Hebrews; it was his insight, determination, and faith that kept the people together. In particular, Moses was the one who brought Yahweh, the God of the covenant, to the people.

The deliverance from Egypt convinced the Hebrews of Yahweh's concern for their welfare. Their memories centered on a narrow escape from Egyptian forces that was made possible by the receding of the waters near the head of the Red Sea (probably in one of the shallow lakes in that area; more accurately they crossed the "Reed Sea"). In any event, it was their conviction that God's hand was seen throughout the difficult period of return to nomadic life on the edge of the desert.

The covenant, or compact of union between Yahweh and the Hebrew people, always remained the central key by which the Hebrews understood their relation to their God. Basic to understanding it was the fundamental point that the covenant was God's gift: their religion was not considered as their way of finding God so much as it was God's way of finding them and offering to them the opportunity for real life. The Hebrews thought of the covenant as a bond between God and the people as a whole. Its demands and its promises were directed to the group rather than to the individual member, and only as a man participated in the life of the group could he share the religion. For a long time the whole social struc-ture of the Hebrews was thought of as standing or falling with its relation to Yahweh. At this time the Hebrews had no thought of life with God after death. Their faith was that God would guide them into a successful and full common life together on earth. The demands of the covenant included both loyalty to Yahweh, to the exclusion of the worship of other gods, and obedience to the commands that made possible the common life of the group. The laws that we now read in Exodus, Leviticus, and Deuteronomy, which formulate these demands, seem to have been expanded and developed as the centuries passed. (See pp. 77-82.)

The forty years of nomadic wanderings centered on the oasis of Kadesh-barnea in southern Palestine. The slave generation passed, giving way to a generation disciplined by the rigors of desert life and inspired by a new religious and national loyalty.

Readings

Exodus 1:1-7:13; 12:29-18:27; 20:1-24:8; 32:1-34:35.
Numbers 10:11-14:45; 20:1-21:35.

Shorter Readings: *Exodus 1:1-3:22; 12:29-15:21; 20:1-17; 24:1-8; 32:1-34:35.*

1. Why did Moses return to Egypt?
2. How was the covenant sealed?
3. What were the terms of the covenant? What did Yahweh promise? What did He demand of the Hebrews?
4. Did only Hebrews escape from Egypt? (Ex. 12:38)
5. Did the sealing of the covenant make the Hebrews firm in their faith in Yahweh?
6. What differences do you see in the terms of the covenant Ex. 20 and Ex. 34? Compare Ex. 20:1-11 with 34:11-22 and 23:17-19 with 34:23-26. What relationship is found in 20:12-17 and 21:1-23:9 that is not in Ex. 34?
7. Is Ex. 33:11 consistent with Ex. 33:21-23? How can the presence of these two points of view about "seeing God" be explained?
8. What qualities are attributed to Yahweh by the writers?
9. Do the writers believe that gods other than Yahweh exist? Do they think of other gods as concerned with or determining the destiny of the Hebrews?
10. Do the writers picture the exodus as the result of a courageous dash for liberty by the enslaved Hebrews? Whom do they picture

as planning and executing the exodus? How does the record suggest that history reveals God? What does it reveal about him? 11. What was Yahweh's purpose in choosing the Hebrews?

Read one of the following:

Wright and Filson, *Westminster Atlas,* rev. ed., pp. 37-39.

Anderson, *Understanding the Old Testament,* pp. 38-59.

Gottwald, *A Light to the Nations,* pp. 115-144.

The Conquest and the Judges

about 1200-1020 B.C.

about 1250-1200 Hebrews enter Canaan
about 1020   Saul becomes the first king of the Hebrews

When the Hebrews entered Palestine, the land was occupied principally by the Canaanites, a people similar to the Hebrews in race and language. There were, however, great differences between the Canaanites and Hebrews in culture and religion.

The Canaanite culture of Syria and Palestine was based on agriculture, but the Canaanites had also developed industry and trade, exporting lumber, textiles, and purple dye. They were a literary people and had developed the first known linear alphabet. Government was aristocratic or feudal; the center of power was the local city or town, in which a small upper class owned the surrounding land and the majority of the population was a subject or serf class which farmed the land. The Canaanite city-states of Syria and Palestine were not effectively united, however, and were often weakened by fighting against each other. Their horse-drawn chariots were a "mechanized" form of warfare that was far more advanced than the tribal "infantry" of the Hebrews.

The book of Joshua pictures Joshua as the great figure of the conquest. It tells how he led the Hebrews into Palestine by way of Jericho and subdued all of the land in one generation. On the other hand, there are indications in the book of Joshua, and especially in Judges, that when Joshua died the Hebrews were settled somewhat precariously in much, but not all, of the central hill country. While the discoveries of modern archeologists have done much to bring the picture of the period into focus, it is still blurred. There is evidence of an invasion of Canaan in the latter half of the thirteenth century. Some of the people in the central hill country seem to have welcomed the Hebrews, and the conquest became a gradual process of infiltration and amalgamation. Alliances were formed with tribes already settled in the land. Battles were fought only when necessary. Slowly, over a period of two centuries, Israel supplanted the Canaanites. On the broad southern part of the coastal plain, the Philistines, who had settled there during the same period, remained strong, so many of the stronger Canaanite cities were not conquered.

The Canaanite religion centered in the cycle of the seasons. Their gods were gods of fertility. The chief god was El, who, with his consort Asherah, ruled over the other gods. But the vital interest of their faith centered on the young god Baal, the god of vegetation, who was thought to come in life-giving power with the spring and to die with the killing heat and dryness of the Palestinian summer. The union of Baal with his sister-wife Anath, or Ashtart, was a symbol of the fertility and productivity of the land. This union was celebrated by imitative rituals in which the divine union was paralleled by "sacred marriage" and other rites in the Baal sanctuaries. Thus Canaanite religion united man's striving to live and reproduce with a divine-cosmic process of life, but it did not contain the clear demand for obedience that was central in the worship of Yahweh, nor did it find the coming of God to man in history.

During the long years of the conquest the Hebrews adopted the agricultural civilization of the Canaanites. They learned to till the soil and to live in houses and towns. But they resisted the religion of Canaan. In fact, loyalty to the God of the covenant was the definitive mark of Israel. They became a group of tribes bound together by devotion to Yahweh and by common service to Yahweh at a common shrine. This kind of tribal league is called an amphictyony, and its unity does not come from a central authority, such as a king, but depends entirely on the strength of a common faith practiced at a common shrine. As a result, Israel could not function as a nation in time of crisis. When from time to time they were threatened, they depended on leaders who rose to the occasion. Such charismatic leaders, believed to be specially inspired, were called judges. Their authority lay in the conviction that they had been "called" by Yahweh. The people fought for Yahweh. Victory convinced them that Yahweh, "The Lord of Hosts," had fought with them. Defeat was interpreted as showing that the people had done "that which was evil in the sight of the Lord."

At the end of the period of conquest, the Hebrews had adopted much of the Canaanite civilization, but they had also rejected much. They had learned to plant and reap—but small farms and relative equality of Hebrew freemen was the usual pattern, not the feudal estates of Canaanite society. They belonged to tribes and towns, but decisions were made by the elders and tribal councils of freemen, not by kings. There were rivalries between tribes, but they were unified in the amphictyony as the Canaanite towns never were. The cult of Baal had influenced their rites, but the gods of fertility had been rejected even while agriculture was being adopted. They still worshipped Yahweh, whose demands were ethical as well as cultic. Palestine had come to be thought of as "the heritage of the Lord," and His covenant still promised that His people should possess the land.

Readings

Joshua 1:1-12:24; 23:1-24:33. Judges 1:1-10:5;
11:1-16:31. I Samuel 4:1-6:16.

Shorter Readings: *Joshua 1:1-9:27. Judges 2:6-10:5.*
I Samuel 4:1-6:16.

1. Who sinned in taking booty from Jericho? Whom did Yahweh punish? How? Whom did Israel punish? How?
2. What attributes qualified one to be a judge in Israel?
3. What powers were attributed to the Ark?
4. According to these books, what is the Yahweh's goal for His people?
5. What parallels to the stories about Moses do you find in the stories about Joshua?
6. State in your own words the understanding of history found in Judges 2:6-3:6.
7. State in your own words the underlying view about responsibility for obedience to Yahweh.
8. Compare Judges 4 and 5. Which version of this story is closer to the event? Why?
9. Compare Joshua 11:16-23 with Joshua 15:63; 16:10; 17:12, and Judges 1:1.
10. Compare Joshua 10:38-39 with Joshua 15:14-17 and Judges 1:11-13.

11. From your reading, do you see any different sorts of traditions on the basis of which these books have been written?

12. Do you see any ways in which later thinking has shaped the telling of the story?

Read one of the following:

Anderson, *Understanding the Old Testament,* pp. 60-121.

Gottwald, *A Light to the Nations,* pp. 145-179.

Wright and Filson, *Westminster Atlas,* rev. ed., pp. 39-44.

The United Kingdom

1020-922 B.C.

1020	*Formation of the kingdom under Saul*
1000	*David becomes king of Judah*
998	*David becomes king of all Israel*
961	*Solomon succeeds David*
922	*Division of the kingdom at Solomon's death*

The growing pressure from enemies, particularly the powerful Philistines of the coastal plain, forced the Hebrews to accept a more unified form of organization, the monarchy. Saul, the first king, was dependent on the cooperation of the tribes, since no centralized form of administration had yet been developed. His army was a people's army of volunteers. At first he was successful, both in the Transjordan against the Ammonites and in the highlands against the Philistines; but he could not permanently drive off the latter. His clash with Samuel shows how the new type of leadership provoked strong resistance from the representatives of the old, and no doubt weakened Saul's authority. His black moods, vividly shown in the stories of his jealousy of David, also made him less effective as a leader. Saul and his able son Jonathan were killed in a disastrous defeat at Mt. Gilboa, by which the Philistines regained control of most of the central hill country.

David, who came from the southern tribe of Judah, had become a popular leader under Saul and married a daughter of the king. He had been driven by Saul first into an outlaw life in the wild country near the Dead Sea, and then into active service under the Philistine king of Gath. After Saul's death David became king of

Judah, making his capital at Hebron. Saul's son Ish-baal attempted to lead the northern tribes, but his rule was weak and ineffective and ended in his murder. David soon established himself as the acknowledged ruler of all the Hebrew tribes. He captured Jerusalem from the Canaanites, who still held it, and made it (a midpoint between Judah and the northern tribes) the capital city. As such it belonged to the king and not to any of the tribes. David fortified Jerusalem and brought to it the Ark of the Covenant to make it a religious center. The Ark, a portable shrine, carried memories of the earlier nomadic days, and David did not replace it with a temple.

David was strikingly successful in his military campaigns, breaking the power of the Philistines in the coastal plain and subduing various groups across the Jordan. Egypt and the kingdoms to the north and east were weak at this time. Thus David built up an empire that controlled the territory and trade of the western end of the Fertile Crescent. He extended Hebrew power over the largest area it reached in the whole of Hebrew history.

David's military force included not only the citizens' army on which Saul had relied, but also professional, paid soldiers who were mostly foreigners and thus not involved in tribal jealousies. He organized a court with powerful administrative officials, thus displacing the power of the tribal leaders. He formed alliances with neighboring nations. However, the reluctance of the Hebrews to accept the monarchy is shown by the difficulties David had in effecting the appointment of his successor. Even though no real attempt was made to return to the purely tribal organization, many felt that the people should have more voice in the affairs of the kingdom. David's son Absalom capitalized on popular discontent and nearly displaced David; the account of this struggle forms one of the masterpieces of historical writing. Later, another son, Adonijah, tried to forestall his father's choice of Solomon.

The peace and prosperity that David established continued under Solomon. Solomon built the magnificent Temple in Jerusalem as part of his group of palace buildings. He organized an elaborate and expensive oriental retinue. Solomon's splendor clashed with the Hebrews' traditions and was bought at the expense of heavy taxes, forced labor, and great debt. At his death, his nation was ripe for revolt.

Hebrew worship was not exclusively centered in Jerusalem, though as time passed the Temple grew in importance and its priests

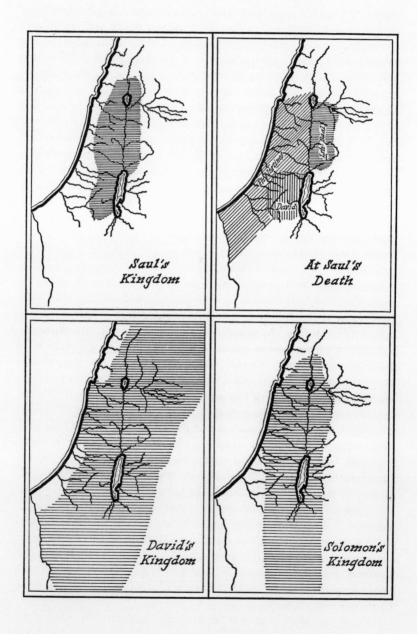

Saul's Kingdom

At Saul's Death

David's Kingdom

Solomon's Kingdom

32

gained a position of preeminence. Sacrifice was the central religious rite, both in the Temple and (until the time of Josiah) in the villages as well. Often understood in paganism as a means of feeding the gods, sacrifice had come to have a quite different meaning for the Hebrews. There were various kinds of sacrifices. One meaning of sacrifice was reconciliation. The worshipper, conscious of his failure to meet God's requirements, offered a life that represented his own, and God accepted this offering as a way of restoring the broken bond. Another meaning of sacrifice was communion. A portion of the animal was burned on the altar and the rest consumed by those who offered the sacrifice. Here the sacrifice was thought of as a bond of fellowship with God. Such sacrifices were often joyful, festive occasions.

During the later period of the Hebrew monarchy, the prophets spoke sharply against the use of sacrifice as a way of avoiding God's demand for moral obedience. Nevertheless, in comparison with the practices of their neighbors, Hebrew worship was distinctive in its honoring the God of the covenant. Though the Hebrews observed festivals in spring and at harvest time, these festivals were very largely memorials of the great events of their history, rather than simply festivals of agriculture. Magic plays almost no part in Hebrew religion. And however weak in practice their faith may have been, the Hebrews believed that God demanded of them an obedience as they lived among their fellow men, an obedience that was closely bound to the honoring of His holiness in worship.

The rule of David and Solomon brought about much greater contact with outside groups, and during this period many signs of borrowing from neighboring faiths appear. The Temple was built on a Phoenician plan. Even in Saul's time and before, names like "Ish-baal" show that many Hebrews thought that there was some similarity between their God and that of their neighbors. In the next period, the time of the divided monarchy, the mixing of Israel's faith with that of the surrounding nations reached the proportions of a major crisis and was strongly resisted by the prophets. Already in the period of the united kingdom we hear of prophets, some of whom, like Nathan who rebuked David for his appropriation of another man's wife, were stern spokesmen for Yahweh, the God who guarantees the standards governing a just life.

Readings

All of I and II Samuel and I Kings 1-11. Read II Samuel 9-20 and I Kings 1-2 as a unit. This is the "Court History of David," which has been called "the first genuine historiography of antiquity."

Shorter Readings: *I Samuel 4:1b-7:2* (see question 2 below) (*A—9:1-10:16; 11:1-15*) (*B—7:3-8:22; 10:17-27; 12:1-25*); *15:1-16:23; 18:1-20:42; 26:1-28:2; 31:1-13. II Samuel 1:1-2:32; 5:1-16; 8:15-18; 11:1-12:25; 15:1-19:43. I Kings 1:1-2:11; 4:1-5:18; 9:10-10:29; 11:41-43.*

1. How would the capture of the Ark by the Philistines stimulate the formation of a kingdom?
2. Read the story of the choice of Saul as king in the order suggested above: first the "A" passages and then the "B" passages.
   a. In the "A" passages, does Samuel welcome the appointment of a king? How is God's will toward a king understood?
   b. In the "B" passages, what is Samuel's attitude toward the appointment of a king? How is God's will toward a king understood?
   c. What is Samuel's title in the "A" passages? What functions belong to that title? What is his title and function in the "B" passages?
   d. Which version of the story is more favorable to Saul? Which version more closely parallels the view of Israel's history found in the book of Judges?
3. What did Saul do when he "prophesied"?
4. What was the cause of Saul's jealousy of David?
5. How did David recruit his outlaw band?
6. Did the people side with Saul or David?
7. How did David win the confidence of both Achish and the Hebrews?
8. What memory of Saul is reflected in David's lament (II Sam. 1:17-27), which probably was written soon after Saul's death?
9. What steps did David take when he heard of Saul's death?
10. How did David capture Jerusalem? Was it a Hebrew city?
11. Describe the organization of David's court.
12. How did Absalom gain support for his revolt?
13. How does the struggle between Adonijah and Solomon reflect a division in David's court?
14. How did the following factors figure in deciding David's successor:
    a. the people's suspicion of a dynastic ruler;
    b. David's tolerant lack of control of his sons;
    c. the traditional antagonism between north and south.

15. What was the nature of Solomon's wisdom?
16. Did Solomon hold all of the territory that David had controlled?
17. Which of these were charismatic leaders: Samuel, Saul, David, Solomon?
18. What source book does I King 11:41 mention?
19. Read I Samuel 12:6-17, Deuteronomy 26:5-10, and Joshua 24:1-15. Note how the memory of God's help is, in each case, brought into the present as the past is relived in a solemn ceremony of dedication. What do these ceremonies suggest about the reasons for and the ways of remembering the past among the Hebrews?

Read one of the following:

Anderson, *Understanding the Old Testament,* pp. 122-153.

Bright, *A History of Israel,* pp. 163-208.

Gottwald, *A Light to the Nations,* pp. 180-233.

Wright and Filson, *Westminster Atlas,* rev. ed. pp. 47-50.

The Divided Kingdom

Israel (922-721 B.C.*)*

922	*Revolt of northern tribes*	842	*Revolt of Jehu*
876	*Omri becomes king*	786	*Jeroboam II becomes king*
869	*Ahab becomes king*	746	*Death of Jeroboam II*
850	*Death of Ahab*	721	*Samaria falls to Assyria*

When Rehoboam, son of Solomon, refused their plea for less oppressive policies, the northern tribes acknowledged the leadership of Jeroboam and established the kingdom of Israel. This northern kingdom overshadowed Judah for the two centuries of its existence. Israel was larger than Judah in territory and population; it had more natural resources and fertile lands; and it was located on the more traveled trade routes. But Israel had no established dynasty (nineteen kings and nine dynasties in 201 years) and no real central shrine. Also, Israel was more open to invasion by Assyria, the rising empire of the day.

A turning-point in the history of the northern kingdom was the rule of Omri, who moved the capital to the city of Samaria, newly built for that purpose. This move put the capital city into closer contact with the kingdoms to the north than it had previously been.

Omri's military successes restored much of the territory across the Jordan which had been lost by his predecessors. He cemented relations with the Phoenicians by marrying his son Ahab to the Phoenician princess Jezebel.

Ahab's rule was not as successful politically as his father's had been, and he was killed in a battle against the forces of Damascus, the perennial enemy of Israel. Ahab's wife, Jezebel, was an able and aggressive worker for the culture and religion of the Phoenicians. She brought in hundreds of "prophets of Baal," and this frontal invasion of a religion substantially like Canaanite religion made great headway. The movement was challenged by the prophet Elijah, whose stern rebuke of Jezebel's judicial murder of Naboth was paralleled by his challenge to the prophets of Baal on Mt. Carmel. Elijah's successor, Elisha, seems to have given his approval to the bloody revolution, some years after Ahab's death, by which Jehu wiped out all the remaining members of Ahab's family (including Jezebel) and the professional adherents of Baal. After this there was no threat of the direct replacement of Yahweh by other gods, though the worship of Baal and other deities continued to creep into the life of the Hebrews alongside the worship of Yahweh, often even in the name of Yahweh.

Jehu's great-grandson, Jeroboam II, once more restored success and prosperity to the northern kingdom, but during his reign Amos, the first prophet whose message was collected in a book, denounced the nation's social corruption and disloyalty to Yahweh. Shortly after the death of Jeroboam II the kingdom of Assyria began its final massive expansion, which swallowed up the kingdom of Damascus in 735 and in 721 engulfed Samaria after a bitter three-year siege of the city.

Readings

I Kings 12-22. II Kings 1-15; 17.

Shorter Readings: *I Kings 12:1-31; 15:25-32; 17:1-19:21; 21:1-29; 22:1-40. II Kings 9:1-10:36; 13:22-14:29; 17:1-41.*

1. Why did Israel revolt against Rehoboam?
2. What were some of the reasons for Israel's political instability?
3. What sources are mentioned by the author?
4. What factor or factors in Baal worship made it appealing?

5. What were the political and economic conditions in Israel under Jeroboam II?
6. Compare the story of Naboth's vineyard with the story of Bathsheba.
7. Compare Micaiah (I Kings 22) with Elijah.
8. What did Assyria do to Israel's people after the fall of Samaria?
9. Who lived in Samaria after 721?
10. What examples are there of prophetic influence on the royal succession? of prophetic comment on the conduct of the rulers?
11. What does the author think of as Jehu's virtuous acts? as his sins?
12. Do you find the view of history stated in Judges reflected in Samuel and Kings?

Read one of the following:

Anderson, *Understanding the Old Testament,* pp. 188-227.

Bright, *A History of Israel,* pp. 209-287.

Gottwald, *A Light to the Nations,* pp. 234-273.

Wright and Filson, *Westminster Atlas,* rev. ed., pp. 50-55.

Judah (922-587 B.C.)

922	*Israel revolts*	626	*Scythian invasion threatens*
735	*Ahaz becomes king*	621	*Reform of Josiah*
735	*Syro-Ephraimitic War*	609	*Death of Josiah*
715	*Hezekiah becomes king*	598	*First capture of Jerusalem*
701	*Siege of Jerusalem by*		*by Nebuchadnezzar*
	Sennacherib	587	*Fall of Jerusalem to*
687	*Manasseh becomes king*		*Nebuchadnezzar*
640	*Josiah becomes king*		

Judah was overshadowed by Israel most of the time from 922 to 721. Judah was smaller in area, less fertile, and more isolated from the coastal trade routes than was Israel. Frequently the smaller kingdom was subservient to the larger. But Judah had only one dynasty throughout her history, that of David (see II Kings 11:1-20 for the only break in the succession). Also, Judah had the Temple of Solomon and an established priesthood, and this Temple gradually gained in prestige.

Shortly after the division of the kingdom Judah was devastated by the Egyptians, and for some time there was considerable tension between the two Hebrew monarchies. Partly because it was somewhat apart from the main lines of commerce with other nations, the southern kingdom never had to confront so direct an invasion of Canaanite religion as that opposed by Elijah and Elisha. Also, the development of a wealthy trading class took place more slowly in Judah. Nonetheless, the same tendency to develop trade and city life did appear in the southern kingdom and brought with it a disregard for the sterner and simpler ways of Yahweh.

About the time of Jeroboam II in the north, Uzziah re-established a measure of peace and prosperity in Judah. His grandson Ahaz was threatened by a coalition of Israel and Damascus, which had joined for mutual protection from the rising power of Assyria. Ahaz responded to this invasion (the so-called Syro-Ephraimitic War) by calling for help from Assyria and becoming its vassal. The result of this struggle was the destruction of Damascus and the devastation of northern Israel by the Assyrians. Ahaz's son and successor, Hezekiah, worked for a return to the sole worship of Yahweh. During most of his reign he remained in subjection to the king of Assyria, paying his tribute regularly. On the death of Sargon II, the powerful Assyrian king who had completed the subjection of Samaria, Hezekiah joined many of the subjects of Assyria in revolting. The new Assyrian king, Sennacherib, was able to crush the revolts in succession, and in 701 B.C. he besieged Jerusalem. The city was spared and Hezekiah was allowed to remain king of Judah, though he was required to pay a large tribute to Sennacherib.

Hezekiah's son, Manasseh, ruled Judah during the time of greatest Assyrian power. He accepted Assyrian ways and religion, bringing Assyrian symbols into the Temple. But during the reign of his grandson, Josiah, Assyria's power rapidly declined. Josiah was only a boy when he began to rule, and the leaders of Judah who controlled the government reacted against the pro-Assyrian policy of Manasseh. Josiah continued the reassertion of Hebrew traditions, both achieving a brief period of political independence as Assyrian power declined and showing a remarkable devotion to the worship of Yahweh. He extended his power toward Samaria, attempting, it seems, to resurrect the Davidic kingdom. The threat of invasion by the Scythians, a barbarian nomadic group that had entered the Fertile Crescent by crossing the Caucasus Mountains, seems to have been taken as a warning of Yahweh's anger by some in Judah, including perhaps the prophet Jeremiah. Not long after this threat a book of law was found in the Temple. This book became the basis of Josiah's reform. The most striking feature of the reform was the putting an end to local altars of sacrifice and the centralizing of all sacrificial worship in the Temple at Jerusalem. (For the reasons for thinking that this book was substantially the book of Deuteronomy, see pp. 78-82.) Josiah was remembered for his loyalty to the cult of Yahweh, including his devotion to the moral demands of the covenant. His death at the hands of the Egyptians brought an end to the career of the last outstanding king of Judah. His four successors were torn between the desire for independence and the necessity of making terms with the great powers, especially the rising power of Babylonia. Nebuchadnezzar, leader of the new Babylonian empire, captured Jerusalem in 598 B.C. and exiled several thousand leading citizens. The last king, Zedekiah, was pushed by popular restlessness into revolt, and Jersualem fell to Nebuchadnezzar again in 587, this time to be destroyed. A second deportation to Babylon took place, and with this destruction came the end of the Davidic monarchy.

Readings

II Kings 16; 18-25. Isaiah 36-37. Jeremiah 39-41.

Shorter Readings: *II Kings 16:1-20; 18:1-19:37. Isaiah 36:1-37:38. II Kings 21:1-26; 22:1-23:30; 23:31-25:30. Jeremiah 39:1-41:18.*

1. Who first put Judah under the rule of Assyria? Why?
2. According to the Hebrew historians, how was Jerusalem saved from the Assyrians?
3. What gods did Manasseh introduce into Jerusalem?
4. Read how later historians explained the long reign of Manasseh: II Chronicles 33:9-13.
5. Describe the details of Josiah's reform.
6. What nations dominated Judah after the death of Josiah?
7. What sources are quoted by the historian?

Read one of the following:

Anderson, *Understanding the Old Testament,* pp. 252-256.

Bright, *A History of Israel,* pp. 288-319.

Gottwald, *A Light to the Nations,* pp. 327-332.

Wright and Filson, *Westminster Atlas,* rev. ed., pp. 50-56.

The Exile and the Return

587-445 B.C.

587   *Jerusalem destroyed by Nebuchadnezzar*
539   *Babylon falls to Cyrus*
516   *Second Temple completed and dedicated*
445   *Nehemiah's return; the rebuilding of the walls of Jerusalem*

The new Babylonian empire exiled the leading element of Judah in order to discourage resistance. The exiles were settled in good-sized colonies where they could follow their own way of life if they wished. Some were absorbed into the Babylonian population, but many remained faithful to Yahweh. It was with these exiles, rather than with the people who remained in Judah, that the future of the Hebrew faith lay. The prophetic movement continued in exile, notably in Ezekiel and the so-called Second Isaiah. Writings of earlier prophets were collected and edited in exile, as were the historical writings. The laws of the Hebrews were also gathered together and revised (see pp. 82-83). The imprisoned King Jehoiachin, grandson of Josiah, retained a position of respect among the people, and his descendants were leaders of the return. The decisive guidance and leadership of the exiles was not to come from the royal house, however, but from those who gathered and meditated on the traditions of Hebrew faith. They were able to build a community that could hold together without the bond of monarchy.

Cyrus the Persian (as we may call him; originally he was the ruler of the small mountain state of Anshan) gained control of the mountains north of the Fertile Crescent and then conquered Babylon. The Persian empire created by Cyrus soon came to control a larger area than any of the previous oriental empires. Cyrus' policy toward subject peoples was relatively lenient. He permitted the Hebrews to return, if they wished, to their native land. Some, no doubt a minority, took advantage of this opportunity. Though Sheshbazzar and Zerubbabel, descendants of the royal family of David, were among the early leaders of this group, they soon disappeared, and the real leadership of the "restored" Jerusalem passed into the hands of the priests. For a long time those who had returned faced a difficult struggle. They had come back largely because of their intense devotion to Yahweh, yet they were not very favorably received by the more compromising followers of Yahweh whom they found in Palestine. It was fully twenty years after the beginning of the restoration of Jerusalem that the Temple was rebuilt, and this task was completed only after the strenuous urging of two prophets, Haggai and Zechariah, had focused the energies of the people.

For some two-thirds of a century the little community of the faithful struggled to keep Judaism alive in Jerusalem. The city had no walls. Their leadership was weak. Temple worship and keeping "clean" from intermarriage with their neighbors became increasingly difficult. The faith was faltering when, about 445 b.c., Nehemiah, a patriotic Jew, left the Persian king's service to help his native city. Nehemiah returned to Jerusalem and enlisted the citizens in the project of rebuilding the city wall. The wall was a necessity in those days if the town was to be a secure and stable center of social and economic life; and it was doubly essential if Jerusalem was to be the focus of a distinctive and not always popular religious community. Under Nehemiah's leadership the wall was completed in a remarkably short time. He thus laid the foundation for a firm structure of civil government. Persian policy permitted a great deal of local freedom to the various religious groups within the empire, and the Jewish community of Palestine was able at last to live in its own way without interference. Nehemiah's work is also interesting in that, though neither a member of a royal family nor a priest, he thought it important to write the story of his own life.

At the same general period as Nehemiah (slightly earlier according to a date in the book of Ezra, but many students hold that this date has become confused, and that Ezra followed Nehemiah) the scribe or scholar Ezra came from Babylonia to Palestine. He persuaded the citizens of Jerusalem to adopt the completed Law as their official standard of religious and community life. Both Ezra and Nehemiah put great emphasis on the sharp separation between Jew and non-Jew, which they thought essential if Judaism was to keep its distinctiveness. The work of Ezra and Nehemiah marked the turning point by which the small and struggling community of Jews in Palestine became firmly established. From this time onward the Law became more and more the standard followed by all Jews—though there were Jews in Egypt and elsewhere who did not follow the full Law as we know it, and in Palestine itself there continued to be worshippers of the God of the Jews whose law differed from that of Jerusalem. These latter, who had tried to check Nehemiah, were the forerunners of the "Samaritans," who accepted a different version of the law and centered their worship at Mt. Gerizim in Samaria. In spite of these variations, the law provided a firmness and unity that kept Judaism together through the centuries.

Readings

i

Jeremiah 52:1-30. Ezra 1:1-11; 3:1-6:22. Haggai 1:1-15. Zechariah 8:2-23. Malachi 1:6-12; 2:10-16. Nehemiah 1:1-6:19; 8:1-9:38; 13:1-31.

1. Were all the inhabitants of Jerusalem taken into exile?
2. Were the Jews able to retain their own religion in exile?
3. Who permitted the exiles to return?
4. Why would the returned Jews not allow other worshippers of Yahweh to aid in rebuilding the Temple?
5. Why did the rebuilding of the Temple go slowly?
6. Contrast the bases on which Haggai and Zechariah pleaded for the rebuilding of the Temple.
7. What practices does Malachi (ca. 450 B.C.) condemn?
8. Note the difficulties Nehemiah overcame to rebuild the walls of Jerusalem.
9. How did he organize for defense and building at the same time?
10. What social reforms did he order at once?
11. How long did it take to restore the walls?
12. What did Nehemiah expect God to do for him? for the people?
13. How was the book of the law presented to the people?
14. How was it ratified by them?
15. How long did it take to read the law to the people?

Read one of the following:

Anderson, *Understanding the Old Testament,* pp. 357-381.

Bright, *A History of Israel,* pp. 323-375.

Gottwald, *A Light to the Nations,* pp. 372-375 and 427-436.

Wright and Filson, *Westminster Atlas,* rev. ed., p. 56.

ii

Lamentations 1:1-5:22.

1. Why would these poems be attributed to Jeremiah?
2. To what causes do the poets attribute Jerusalem's downfall?

3. Is Yahweh responsible for the evil that has come upon His people?
4. Does Lamentations 5:7 reflect a corporate or an individual understanding of guilt?

Obadiah 1:1-20 (see also p. 74).

5. Who refused to help the Hebrews in their struggle with Nebuchadnezzar?
6. Contrast the spirit of Obadiah with that of Lamentations.
Anderson, *Understanding the Old Testament,* p. 447.

Psalm 137.

7. What period does this Psalm reflect?
8. Show how verses 1-6 parallel Lamentations and verses 7-9 parallel Obadiah.
Gottwald, *A Light to the Nations,* pp. 512, 513.

iii

Ruth 1:1-4:22.

1. How can this book be understood as a gentle rebuke to the point of view represented by Nehemiah? (Note Ruth 4:17-22 and Nehemiah 13:24-30.)
Anderson, *Understanding the Old Testament,* p. 452.

Post-Exilic Period

445-63 B.C.

From the time of Nehemiah to New Testament times, we have no source book of history in the Protestant canon. In the Apocrypha, there are two books of history that cover one brief period. These are I and II Maccabees, which tell the story of the Jewish revolt from Syrian rule in the second century B.C. Besides these two books, the principal source for Jewish history in the post-exilic period is the writings of Josephus, a Jewish historian who wrote in Rome at the end of the first century A.D.

Briefly, the history of the Jewish community in Palestine after 445 B.C. can be outlined as follows:

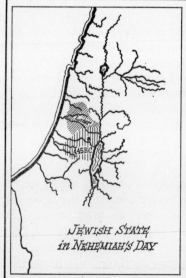

LEGEND:
Assyrian
Babylonian
Persian

ANCIENT EMPIRES

Europe

Black Sea

Caspian Sea

Mediterranean Sea

Asia

Africa

ARABIA

Nile River

Red Sea

Persian Gulf

JEWISH STATE
in NEHEMIAH'S DAY

The MACCABEAN
KINGDOM

445-333 B.C. For a century, the Jerusalem community prospered. In local affairs it was practically independent. The community was small (perhaps fifty miles by twenty-five, population 100,000) but secure. Jerusalem was protected by the newly built wall. The community was ruled by the priests, with the law as "constitution." Persia was tolerant and preserved the peace.

Sometime during the century, Persia's tolerance became laxness and inefficiency, but the results did not touch the Jews until about 350 B.C., when some of Judah's neighbors revolted from Persia and were ruthlessly subdued. Judah also suffered in this fighting, in which the Persian empire was greatly weakened.

333-198 B.C. Alexander crushed the weakened Persians in 333. His enormous conquests were far more than military ventures, for he believed that he had a mission to spread Greek culture. By his technique of founding Greek cities he greatly hastened the spread of Greek culture in the Orient. Alexander died in 323, but Greek culture continued to fuse with that of the Near East. His empire broke up—Egypt going to the Ptolemies and Syria to the Seleucids. Palestine was ruled by the Ptolemies during most of the third century B.C. and was treated fairly well. Jews served as soldiers in the Egyptian armies and founded colonies in Egypt.

The high priest, advised by a council of leading citizens, ruled Judea. The Temple stood as the great leading shrine toward which Jews of the dispersion (or diaspora) as well as those of Judea turned for the great festivals and sacrificial rites. The synagogue, a local assembly for worship and other purposes, spread with the dispersion throughout the world. It was dedicated to the Law and to the worship of God through knowledge and observance of the Law.

But the Law was not all of the great literature of Judaism, and the reverence for the Sacred Book grew during this period to include the Prophets. By the end of the third century B.C. the canon was the Law and the Prophets—and the prophets were divided into the "former prophets" (the historical books) and the "latter prophets" (the prophetic writings). Of course new works were also written during the Greek period. Probably from this time come I and II Chronicles, a retelling of the history of the united kingdom and Judah by a priestly writer, as well as the Song of Songs, a collection of love poetry or wedding songs that was eventually canonized because it was attributed to Solomon and because it was interpreted allegorically.

Greek was the language of commerce and scholarship, and many Jews of the dispersion knew only Greek. During the third century the translation of the Hebrew Scriptures into Greek began—a work performed at Alexandria, and probably in its beginning intended for use in the synagogues of Jews who knew no Hebrew. The Greek translation of the Old Testament, known as the Septuagint, made Judaism better known in the pagan world and was later adopted by the Christians as their Old Testament.

198-63 B.C. In 198 B.C. the Seleucid ruler of Syria, Antiochus III ("the Great"), captured Palestine from the Ptolemies. The conflict between the Hellenistic and the Jewish ways came to a head during the reign of Antiochus IV ("Epiphanes"). Antiochus not only interfered with the high priesthood and temple revenues, but also tried to force his own combination of Greek and Near Eastern culture and religion upon the Jews and to stop the Jews from following their particular faith. The conflict reached its height in 167 B.C., when Antiochus' forces occupied the Temple, and, putting an end to Jewish worship there, set up an image to Zeus (the "desolating abomination" of Daniel 11:31). Antiochus persecuted Judaism wherever he could find it, trying to make the Jews give up their distinctive faith. Among the Near Eastern cultures, Judaism was the only one that vigorously resisted the penetration of Greek culture. Jewish monotheism could not accommodate itself to the Greek culture, which did not base itself on reverence for the One God; and while the new culture was attractive to many Jews, most of them found the object of their highest loyalty to be the Law. The book of Daniel comes from this period, in the opinion of most Protestant scholars, and reflects both the history of the struggle and the spirit of resistance to persecution.

Resistance to Antiochus centered around the priest Mattathias and his sons. Mattathias sparked the revolt by refusing to sacrifice to Zeus and killing a compatriot who was willing to do so. His sons led a guerrilla resistance for several years. The chief of these sons was Judas, often called Judas Maccabeus ("the Hammerer"). In 164 B.C. Judas and his followers forced Antiochus to permit the rededication of the Temple, and freedom to practice Judaism was gained once more. But religious freedom did not end the conflict. During twenty years of intermittent warfare the Jews continued their struggle with the Seleucids, led by Judas until his death, and later by Jonathan and then Simon, brothers of Judas. Finally, in 142 B.C.,

Simon expelled the Seleucid garrison from Jerusalem, and this date is usually taken to mark the political freedom of the Jews. Once more they had become an independent nation. Simon's descendants, called the Hasmoneans or Maccabees, ruled this Jewish state until 63 B.C. These rulers combined political power (eventually assuming the title "king") with the high priesthood. During the first fifty years of its existence the Hasmonean kingdom grew to include Samaria, Galilee, and a considerable strip of the land across the Jordan. The political success of the Hasmoneans led to the growth of a vigorous religious patriotism. Forced conversions to Judaism were one feature of Jewish expansion—as in many other cases, the struggle for their own religious freedom had not made the leaders sensitive to the need of others for freedom to practice their faith. The book of Esther is an expression of Jewish patriotism, bitter in its hatred of oppressors, probably written during the period of Maccabean expansion, not long before 100 B.C. Another reaction to Jewish political success was disapproval and withdrawal of support for the Hasmoneans by many of the deeply religious Jewish leaders. The increasing concern of the rulers for political power led the "Hasidim," or pious, to emphasize a religion that was not political in expression, but forced rather on quiet obedience to the Law in a separate community. The Quamran community, from which the Dead Sea Scrolls come, represents an extreme form of reaction against the secularization of religious leadership by the Hasmoneans.

The last years of the Hasmonean or Maccabean state were marred by a civil war, which led to intervention by Rome. In 63 B.C. the Jews lost their independence to the Romans, though one of the Hasmonean line continued for a time as high priest (see Chap. 10).

Readings

Read one of the following:

Anderson, *Understanding the Old Testament,* pp. 430-537.

Bright, *A History of Israel,* pp. 389-445.

Gottwald, *A Light to the Nations,* pp. 495-503; 533-537.

Wright and Filson, *Westminster Atlas,* rev. ed., pp. 77-84.

5

The Prophets

The prophets are the turning point of the Old Testament. They bring into sharpest focus the claim for obedience in the covenant faith, and at the same time they look forward to a new act of God, so that the future as well as the past comes into the perspective of faith.

To us "prophet" means someone who can foretell the future. We speak of "political prophets" and "weather prophets." The Old Testament prophets were concerned with the future—but they were not at all concerned with providing a blueprint of future events, as if all things were determined in advance. "Prophet" to them meant "spokesman for God," a man whom God had chosen as the agent through whom His purpose was declared. The future of which they spoke was for them not the unfolding of the human story, but the decisive encounter of the people with the holy God.

We read of prophets as early as the time of Saul and David. Most of these early prophets were "ecstatic" prophets who believed that they spoke for God when they were in a state of emotional frenzy (see, for example, I Samuel 10:9-12). They usually encouraged a narrow, nationalistic type of faith. Others, however, were courageous and often lonely spokesmen for God who represented and deepened the best claim of the covenant faith. Such men were Nathan (II Samuel 12), Elijah (I Kings 21), and Micaiah (I Kings 22:1-40; this story is a good example of both types of prophets).

As far as we know, Amos was the first prophet whose messages were preserved in a book. From as early as the ninth century, stories of prophets were remembered in some detail (the Elijah and Elisha stories). Stories about the prophets are found in the great prophetic books as well. But the books of the prophets are mainly collections of short poems in which the prophets expressed the "word" of God which had come to them. Both the sacred and the secular poetic forms of their day were put to the service of their message. At the center of their speech were the poems in which God Himself spoke to the people, usually in threat, sometimes in encouragement. Even when the prophet spoke in his own name, his word was not part of a general system of religious truths, but was a formulation of the "word" that God was speaking through him to the people and to the situation that he confronted.

Prophetic religion, like the preceding covenant faith, makes its primary concern the people of God. That God had chosen a special people, set them aside for His purpose, and given them a covenant by which they could know Him and respond to His purpose—these were assumptions of the prophets, though they interpreted the claim of this covenant much more radically than had been done before their time. They saw God at work in the common daily life of man, in his family and work, in the events of nature, and especially in the common life of the people. The community existed in order to be the kind of community God wanted it to be, and He was constantly at work to make it what it ought to be, or, if necessary, to punish it for failing.

Amos and the prophets who followed him set forth their sharpened understanding of the Hebrew faith in the face of historical crises that seemed to be destroying not only the faith, but also the very existence of the Hebrews. The time of the great prophets was the time of the Assyrian and Babylonian domination of Palestine. The prophets were able to see these catastrophic years as ruled by Yahweh and not as a sign of His abandoning His people.

The recurring theme of the prophets is doom. The Hebrews have been disloyal to God's demand for obedience; they have neglected the great opportunity He has set before them of becoming His people and have tried to live out of their own resources. But man cannot ultimately live out of his own resources, and God cannot tolerate such disloyalty. Therefore He is about to destroy the Hebrew society, using as His instrument the destructive power of some invasion. In this message there is little speculation about monotheism, though it is always assumed that Yahweh is the only God to be taken into account. Nor is there any concern to develop a practical plan of reform that will cure the abuses in society and cult. The prophets simply speak forth the just will of God, which cannot endure disloyalty or corruption, and which will destroy the corrupt and disloyal people.

In almost every case, however, there is another side to the message of the prophet. God's justice demands that the people be punished—but His original generous purpose of creating a good community will not fail. Because of their faith in the profound and persistent goodness of God, the prophets saw hope of a new life beyond the punishment. The new life they described in various ways, but they did not think of the future as a life after death in the presence of God.

Thus, unlike most great religious books, the Old Testament has an element of incompleteness. The prophets held that God had not yet done all that He would do. The future holds something greater than has thus far been disclosed. Christians saw these hopes fulfilled in Christ. It is natural and right that Christians should emphasize this aspect of the prophetic teaching, but it must be seen in its setting in the prophetic message as a whole. Christians have done violence to both Testaments when they have read the prophetic writings with an eye for nothing except those passages that could be interpreted as predictions of some incident recorded in the New Testament. God is sovereign over the life of man; there is no real security in the constructions of man's society and culture, but only in faith in the living God; God is an active force, to be met in the events of life, although the great, totally direct encounter with God lies in the future; God is both just and merciful, insisting on obedience and yet willing and able to create anew after punishment—these are the foundations of the prophetic point of view, and of the point of view of the Bible as a whole.

Readings

The prophets' call: *Isaiah 6:1-13. Amos 7:14-15; 3:3-8 (also 7:1-9; 8:1-3; 9:1-4) Jeremiah 1:1-19; 15:15-21. Ezekiel 1:1-3:11. Isaiah 40:3-8.*

1. Did the prophets understand themselves as talking about God or as participating in God's action?
2. Did these men deliberately plan and prepare to become prophets?
3. Did they think of their prophesying as an expression of their free wills or an expression of God's will?
4. How did they explain their continuing in the face of unconcern, opposition, and persecution?
5. How did they understand their relation to God? to the people?

The prophets' word and action: (a) *Amos 4:1-12 (note 3:1 and 5:1). Hosea 4:1-6; 8:1-10. Isaiah 1:1-11, 24-26. Note Jeremiah 1:4, 9, 11, 13; 2:1, 4 and Ezekiel 3:4-11.*

1. Note how the ancient world thought of a "word" as having power.
2. Did the prophets think of their words as being their "word" or Yahweh's?
3. Did they think of themselves as discoverers of general truths or channels for concrete revelation for a specific situation?

(b) *Hosea 1:2-5; 3:1-5. Isaiah 20:1-6. Jeremiah 13:1-11. Ezekiel 4:1-17.*

1. Did the prophet think of his actions as "illustrations" or as embodiments of the power of Yahweh?
2. Compare with the tenth century prophet of I Kings 11:29-31.

The prophets and the future: *Amos 3:12-15; 5:18-20. Hosea 5:13-6:6. Micah 3:1-12. Isaiah 1:24-26; 2:12-22; 10:1-11; 30:15-18. Jeremiah 8:4-12; 15:5-9. Ezekiel 15:1-8. Isaiah 40:1-31; 45:1-8.*

1. What relation did the prophets see between the present and the future?
2. Study the interplay between divine purpose and human decision in these passages.
3. Why must the prophetic message emphasize judgment? Why cannot the prophetic message be limited to the word of judgment?
4. As observers of history, were the prophets interested in international relations, alliances, or military power, the strength of the empires, or Israel's "image"?
5. State the course of action that the prophets urged on their people in their relations with other nations. What is the relation of this

course of action to what we call an "international policy"? What are the presuppositions about the community from which the prophets spoke? Do you see their message as in any way relevant to the present-day situation?

The covenant and exodus: *Amos 2:9-11; 3:1-2. Hosea 2:14-15; 11:1-9; 12:13-14. Jeremiah 3:19-20; 11:1-5; 31:27-34. Isaiah 51:9-11.*

1. What act of God did these prophets understand to be the ground for Israel's faith?
2. What did they consider to be the primary demand of the covenant?
3. How did they interpret their times in relation to the deliverance and the covenant?
4. In what sense is the covenant still a basis for hope?

The preservation of the prophetic word: *Isaiah 8:16-18; 30:8-17. Jeremiah 36:1-32.*

1. What indications do we find here as to how and why the prophetic words were remembered and recorded?

Read one of the following:

Anderson, *Understanding the Old Testament,* pp. 183-188.

Dodd, *The Bible Today,* Chap. 3.

Gottwald, *A Light to the Nations,* pp. 273-281.

The Interpreter's Bible, Vol. I, pp. 292-348.

Amos

Amos (ca. 750 B.C.), a shepherd from Tekoa in southern Judah, came from an area in which the simple but stern morality of the nomad was still influential. His public activity took place entirely in the northern kingdom. In his time Israel was enjoying peace and prosperity under Jeroboam II. (See the historical outline, p. 36.) But the nobles and commercial classes used the power of money and the control of the courts to reduce the independent farmer to serfdom. At the same time the worship of Yahweh, influenced by the colorful rites of Baal, had grown into an elaborate ritual, so that the claim of the covenant to obedience in man's relation to his fellow man was obscured.

Amos thought of Yahweh as a universal, righteous God. He

assumed that Yahweh would punish neighboring nations for their crimes, even if not committed against the Hebrews. Yet the righteousness of God had been specifically made known to the Hebrews, and it was in encounter with them both in the past and in the future and not in "history in general" that Amos saw God at work.

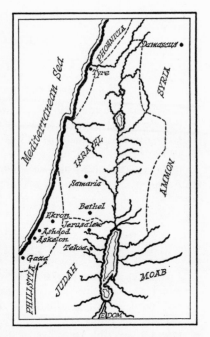

Amos assumed that Yahweh had chosen the Hebrews and that their covenant relationship with God placed a unique responsibility on them. He mentioned God's guidance of the history of the Syrians, Philistines, and others; but the Hebrews were distinguished by the fact that they could know Yahweh as other nations could not, and God expected them to respond accordingly.

Amos' pungent attacks on the social injustice that he saw— bribery in the courts, cheating and false weights in the market place, the heartless way in which the rich enjoyed their easy life without concern for the less fortunate—convinced him that the Hebrews had rejected their covenant opportunity. He saw no possible outcome except immediate and overwhelming destruction. He understood a series of previous small-scale disasters as warnings, warnings that had been ignored. Thus the great, final meeting with God must come, and it would be a disaster, the end, for the people. Whereas the traditional faith understood the punishments threatened in the covenant as applying to the group or individual who sinned, Amos understood them as turned against the whole people.

There were a few places where he spoke a "perhaps," a "perhaps" that God would be gracious to the people, after only a fragment of them was left. This "perhaps" was strongly developed into a message of hope at the end of the book, which may be a later addition (see below, Section x).

Readings

i

Read the book of Amos.

1. Locate on the map the town and country in which Amos lived, the town and country in which he preached.
2. How was Amos received? Why?
3. Why did Amos deny that he was a prophet? What did the priest mean by "prophesy and eat bread"?
4. Note how Amos' figures of speech reflect his rural background.

ii

Amos 1:1-2:8.

1. Locate on the map the countries Amos condemned.
2. What were the specific sins of these countries? What was the general nature of their sins? Did Amos' hearers consider these acts sinful?
3. Of what sin did Amos accuse Judah?
4. Of what sins did Amos accuse Israel? How did these differ from the sins he had mentioned up to this time?
5. In the light of 5:14 do you think his hearers looked on their conduct as sinful?
6. In a sentence, what is the main theme of this sermon?

iii

Amos 4:4-5[1]; 5:4-5; 5:21-27.

1. Did Amos accuse Israel of failing to offer sacrifices, pay tithes, or observe feasts, fasts, and Sabbaths?
2. What attitude did he condemn in 4:5?
3. Did he repudiate the ritual or call for its purification? Defend your stand.
4. What is the meaning of 5:25? Can you harmonize this with Leviticus 1-7? Compare with Jeremiah 7:21-23.
5. Note 5:26. Did Amos emphasize the sin of idolatry?

[1] Bethel and Gilgal were shrines to Yahweh.

iv

Amos 2:6-8; 4:1-3; 5:10-13; 6:4-8; 8:4-6.

1. List the specific acts condemned by Amos.
2. Classify these acts into general categories. Where did Amos lay the greatest stress?
3. Did the priesthood of Amos' day consider these practices sinful? (Note 7:10-17.)
4. Whom was Amos condemning in 4:1-3?
5. Why did Amos deplore luxuries?

v

Amos 4:6-12.

1. Had Yahweh called Israel to repentance? How?
2. For Amos, what did history reveal about Yahweh?
3. Did Amos speak of the individual or the nation as responsible to Yahweh?

vi

Amos 2:13-16; 3:9-15; 5:1-3; 5:16-17; 6:6-7; 8:7-14; 9:1-8a.

1. What means would Yahweh use to punish Israel?
2. Is there any note of hope in these passages?
3. Did Amos predict the punishment of the rich and powerful only?
4. Would the judgment extend to the whole nation or only to a certain part of it?

vii

Amos 2:9-12; 3:2; 9:7.

1. Did Amos accept the idea that Israel has a unique relationship with Yahweh?
2. The people felt that the covenant gave them privileges that other people did not have. How did Amos reinterpret this concept of the covenant?

viii

Amos 5:18-20.

1. What does this passage imply as to the popular hope of the Day of the Lord?
2. How did Amos reinterpret it?

ix

Amos 7:1-9.

1. Note that Amos did not protest the third vision of destruction. On the contrary, he went out to preach destruction. Would you explain this as the loss of his original concern for Israel or as a new understanding of God's reasons for destruction?
2. What does the plumb-line symbolize?

x

Amos 9:1-15.

1. At what point in this chapter does the prediction of destruction give way to a prediction of restoration?
2. In 9:9-10, who is responsible to Yahweh, the nation or the individual?
3. In 9:11, what is to be restored? What relation did the Israel of Amos' day have with it? Was it in ruins in Amos' day?
4. What is the reason for this change?

Read one of the following:

Anderson, *Understanding the Old Testament,* pp. 228-237.

Bewer and Kraeling, *Literature of the Old Testament,* pp. 89-96.

Buber, *The Prophetic Faith,* pp. 96-110.

Gottwald, *A Light to the Nations,* pp. 281-291.

Hosea

Hosea (ca. 740 B.C.) was a citizen of the northern kingdom and prophesied there. He was familiar with city life, with the details of priestly religion, and with the political situation. The few years between Amos and Hosea were years of rapid decline in the power and stability of the kingdom of Israel, and Hosea's book reflects the disorders of his time. (See the historical outline, p. 36.)

Hosea is known as the prophet of love, but he did not forget the requirements of justice. His prophecies included repeated mention of crimes of violence, perhaps reflecting the increasing social disorganization of his day. He censured Jehu's murder of the house of

Ahab, which the earlier prophet Elisha had approved. He held that the policy of making alliances with Assyria or Egypt could not bring security to the nation. Hosea placed particular responsibility for national decay on the priests, who (he held) had misled the people into thinking that formal, idolatrous worship was God's real requirement.

While Amos had limited himself largely to observing actions and their consequences, Hosea's message probed more deeply into the sources of the people's sinfulness. Specific sins resulted from instability of character. The people were fickle, disloyal. They did not really believe in anything. "Lack of knowledge" of God was the root of the difficulty. By "knowledge" Hosea meant much more than the abstract "right idea" of God; the people were "out of relation" with God. Consequently, Hosea showed more interest in religious worship than had Amos. Idolatry is condemned many times over, because it stood in the way of a right knowledge of Yahweh.

Hosea expected punishment to fall on the whole people. Like Amos, he did not specify just how or when it would take place. He expected that God would act through the processes of nature and history. But this necessary punishment was not the whole picture. Drawing on the tradition of the covenant, which emphasized the special concern of God for His chosen people, Hosea presented the view that God loved His people even when they did wrong and would restore them when they repented. Here he boldly adopted the symbol of marriage (often avoided because it was associated with Baal religion) to show the relationship between God and His people.

Hosea's intense conviction of God's love was expressed in his own personal life. He dramatically set forth the wrongness of the people's relation to God by marrying a harlot—perhaps a woman who had taken part in the rites of the Temple prostitutes. Later he purchased a common slave (perhaps his wife) and made this act a symbol of God's concern for a sinful people. Though they were disloyal, God still loved His people and wanted to help them, in spite of their not deserving His help. Having this view of God, Hosea emphasized the religious response of loyalty and affection.

Readings

i

Hosea 1:1-9; 3:1-5.

1. Is the wife of Chapter 1 the same as the woman of Chapter 3? What is the reason for your answer?
2. How do you understand the command of God in 1:2?
3. What is the meaning of the reference to Jezreel in 1:4-5? (See II Kings 9:16-28.)
4. Is there any element of hope in the message presented by the symbolic names of the children?

ii

Hosea (a) 4:11-19; 8:4-6; 11:2; 13:2; (b) 5:13; 7:8-16; (c) 4:2; 6:7-9.

1. List the sins Hosea condemned in these pages.
2. List a general category for each group (*a, b, c*).
3. Which category did Hosea emphasize most?
4. Which category is most like Amos?
5. Why did Hosea think group *b* was sinful?

iii

Hosea 2:8; 4:1, 6, 14; 5:4.

1. What reason did Hosea give for Israel's sin?
2. Whom did Hosea particularly blame? (See 4:4-9).

iv

Hosea 5:8-14; 8:11-14; 9:10-17.

1. What will be the result of Israel's sinfulness?
2. Is Hosea's picture as hopeless as Amos'?

v

Hosea 5:15-6:3; 11:1-9; 14:1-3.

1. What is Yahweh's attitude toward sinful Israel?
2. How will Israel react to her coming punishment?

vi

Hosea 11:9-11; 14:4-8.

1. Did Hosea see utter destruction for Israel?
2. Did Hosea repudiate Amos' idea of a just God?
3. If not, how can he picture restoration?

Read one of the following:

Anderson, *Understanding the Old Testament*, pp. 237-251.

Bewer and Kraeling, *Literature of the Old Testament*, pp. 96-102.

Buber, *The Prophetic Religion*, pp. 110-126.

Gottwald, *A Light to the Nations*, pp. 291-305.

Isaiah

Isaiah (ca. 740-700 B.C.) was a citizen of Jerusalem and directed most of his prophecies to the southern kingdom. (See the historical outline, p. 38.) Though he was apparently well-to-do himself, he showed keen sympathy for the poor and underprivileged. His condemnation of social injustice in Judah has much in common with the teaching of Amos. He repeatedly spoke of the administration of justice as the real test of obedience to God. Mere formal acts of worship in religion were vividly condemned by Isaiah as useless. Underlying the deterioration of the community he saw the fundamental difficulty of human pride. The basic sin, from which the others resulted, was arrogance, which ignored the greatness of God.

Isaiah's condemnation of pride went hand in hand with an intense conviction of God's holiness. Holiness, or "mysterious divine power," is what Isaiah encountered in his meeting with God and presented with power in his message. Before Yahweh, man can only acknowledge his sin and littleness in humility. To Isaiah, God's holiness was just and merciful, but man cannot determine what justice and mercy are apart from God, and God alone has power to establish conditions of justice and mercy.

Like Amos and Hosea, Isaiah predicted destruction. In particular, Isaiah accepted the Assyrian expansion and ultimate invasion as God's means of punishment. Thus history was subject to God, and the nations, even though they did not know it, were serving His purposes. In this sense Isaiah emphasized the power of God over nations other than the Hebrews, but he was not interested in seeing a universal plan of history.

Isaiah, like Hosea, held that God's goodness was so great that He would not completely destroy His people. A "remnant" would survive. Perhaps at the start Isaiah's statement that a remnant would survive was a threat—"only a remnant"—but it later became a message of hope. Though God would destroy, He would also rebuild starting with the survivors, who, Isaiah held, would return to God with all their energies. The tradition that Isaiah used and transformed for his message of judgment and hope was not, like that of Hosea, one that rested on the covenant-exodus tradition, but one that looked back to God's action for David and Jerusalem.

A small nation, engaged in a vital struggle to prevent absorption by the great Assyrian empire, would not easily see things as Isaiah did. It was not easy to be sure that Yahweh was in control of events when Assyria seemed to be on the point of blotting out the chosen people. Nevertheless, Isaiah urged the nation's leaders to let their faith in God guide their decisions. The clue to success and security for the nation was not to be found in alliances or military preparations, but in trusting confidence in God and in obedience to His standards. Isaiah's message did not spring from a weighing of practical alternatives, but from a trust in the coming action of God. His emphasis on wholehearted trust has led to his being called the first great prophet of faith.

Readings

i
Isaiah 1:21-23; 3:13-4:1; 5:8-24; 10:1-4.

1. What kinds of sins were most sharply denounced by Isaiah?
2. Was Isaiah's message more like Hosea's or Amos' in this respect?

ii

Isaiah 1:10-17.

1. Did Isaiah share Amos' evaluation of ritual?

iii

Isaiah 2:10-19; 9:8-10:4; 5:25-30[1]; 7:18-25; 8:11-22; 5:1-7.

1. Is his picture of the future comparable to Amos'?
2. What kinds of disasters did he expect? Who would cause them?

iv

Isaiah 1:8-9; 6:13; 10:20-27; 11:11-16.

1. Did Isaiah predict complete destruction?
2. Did he predict national repentance?
3. How would the remnant be selected?
4. Would it be a group of righteous individuals?

v

Isaiah 6:1-9; 5:16, 24; 12:6; 2:17; 13:6; 3:16; 13:11.

1. In Isaiah's vision note the emphasis on God's majesty and holiness and man's unworthiness or "uncleanness."
2. What earthly model was the pattern for the vision of the divine court and the divine presence?
3. How did Isaiah relate the stubborn resistance of the people to the divine purpose?
4. In other passages, note his stress on the holiness of God and on the sin of arrogance.

vi

Isaiah 3:1-15.

1. On whom did Isaiah place the blame for Judah's sinfulness? How did this compare with Hosea?

Isaiah 7:1-9.

2. With whom was Isaiah arguing at this time? When did this incident take place? What policy did Isaiah urge?

Isaiah 7:18-20; 10:5-15.

3. How did Isaiah explain Assyria's success? What did he see as her final status?

[1] In the Smith-Goodspeed translation, this section follows 10:4.

Isaiah 30:1-33; 31:1-3.

4. How did Isaiah ask the leaders and the people to respond to the dangers of their age? Note 30:15 for a particularly clear formulation.

Isaiah 36:1-37:38.

5. What was the response of the people and leaders in the face of the Assyrian invasion?

The book of Isaiah contains several poems in praise of a coming king, a descendant of David, who will establish a reign of peace. Some of these may come from a later time than that of Isaiah; at any rate, the hope for an ideal king and a peaceful kingdom grew much stronger in later times, when the kingdom had been destroyed. Later still, Christians quite naturally understood these poems as prophecies of Christ, since they believed that Christ was the agent (Messiah, or anointed) of God, appointed by God to set up His kingdom. Passages from several other prophets are added in the readings below to illustrate the nature of the hope.

Isaiah 7:10-17.

1. What crisis brought forth this prophecy?
2. Was the birth to take place soon?
3. Why did Ahaz react as he did?
4. Note the application of this passage in Matthew 1:22-23.

Isaiah 9:1-7.

5. What hope is pictured here?
6. What would be the function of the coming ruler?
7. Where would his kingdom be situated?

Isaiah 11:1-9.

8. Compare this with Isaiah 9:1-7.

Isaiah 2:1-4.

9. Compare this with the above and with Micah 4:1-5.

Jeremiah 23:5-6; 33:15-16.

10. Compare this with the hope expressed in the book of Isaiah.

Micah 5:2-4.

11. What were the functions of the ideal ruler?

Zechariah 9:9-10.

12. Compare this section from a much later writing with the above.
13. Summarize the hope expressed in these passages.

Read one of the following:

Anderson, *Understanding the Old Testament,* pp. 259-273.

Bewer and Kraeling, *Literature of the Old Testament,* pp. 103-121.

Buber, *The Prophetic Faith,* pp. 126-154.

Gottwald, *A Light to the Nations,* pp. 308-326.

Jeremiah

Jeremiah (ca. 626-586 B.C.) came from a family of priests in the village of Anathoth, a few miles north of Jerusalem. His call to prophesy came in connection with the break up of the Assyrian empire, the collapse of which both freed Judah temporarily and exposed it to the threat of invasion from the north.

Though his condemnation of social injustice sounds much like Amos or Isaiah, Jeremiah stood particularly in the same tradition as Hosea. His message, like Hosea's, was based strongly on the exodus-covenant tradition and reflected a similar stress on the unfaithfulness of the people to the covenant and the cost to God of this disloyalty. Like the earlier prophets, he predicted destruction—complete destruction as far as Judah itself was concerned.

Living through the period of Josiah's reform, Jeremiah was apparently largely silent about it. He held that the covenant was too thoroughly broken to be restored in this way.

Jeremiah regarded the Babylonian advance as the coming punishment from God. He saw the futility of resistance and advised the people to accept Babylonian rule as the will of God. He saw it as an inevitable punishment for their disloyalty; if they would accept it as such, there might be hope beyond the disaster. Neither the leaders nor the people would accept this judgment, however, and Jeremiah finally concluded that the utter destruction of Judah was the only possibility.

For the exiles he had hope. He encouraged them, and though he did not expect them to return soon, he held out hope for an eventual restoration of Judah. He expected the exiles to remain loyal to Yahweh. Here, as in his advice to surrender to the Babylonians, we see his faith in God's power to create a community bound together by a deeper and more personal bond than that established by the cult and royal traditions.

Through most of his life Jeremiah had few followers. He was a lonely man of tender and affectionate personality. The long experience of isolation threw him back on God. In his writings there is reflected a much more self-conscious personal religion than can be seen in the earlier prophets, though the whole stream of the great prophetic tradition leads toward this self-awareness.

Disillusionment with ritual religion and the monarchy as bases for the unity of the people, combined with deep awareness of God's personal presence, provided the background for the idea of the new covenant. The hope of the new covenant was that God would in the future establish complete individual responsibility, instead of punishing the community as a whole; that He would forgive the sins of the people; and that We would establish a "new covenant," which would be "written in the hearts," that is, each man would personally encounter God and would not be dependent on a formal or written covenant.

Readings

i

Jeremiah 1:1-10; 11:18-23; 16:1-4; 18:18; 19:14-20:6; 21:1-7; 24:1-10; 26:1-24; 27:1-28:17; 29:1-23; 36:1-32; 37:11-21; 38:1-13; 43:1-7.

1. List the events in the life of Jeremiah recorded in these passages.
2. Where was Jeremiah born?
3. Where did he preach?
4. What profession did his family follow?
5. How did his hometown receive him?
6. What enemies did he make? How?
7. How did he interpret the Babylonian advance?

ii

Jeremiah 1:11-19; 4:5-31.

1. How do these prophecies differ from the predictions of destruction found in the eighth-century prophets?

iii

Jeremiah 7:1-8:3; 26:1-24.

1. Of what sins did Jeremiah accuse the people?
2. Were these different from the sins condemned by the eighth-century prophets?
3. Compare 7:21-23 with Amos 5:25. What was the prophets' idea of worship in the wilderness period?
4. Note 8:3. How did Jeremiah reinterpret the doctrine of the remnant?
5. Compare his ideas of the Temple with Isaiah's.
6. Compare the prophecy of Chapter 7 with the narrative about Jeremiah in Chapter 26. What themes appear in both accounts of this episode? Is Chapter 7 concerned with the personal fate of Jeremiah?

iv

Jeremiah 2:4-13; 5:1-17; 8:18-9:16; 9:17-24; 10:17-25; 12:7-13; 13:20-27; 14:17-22; 18:1-17.

1. Read these poems to find why Jeremiah is considered among the great poets.
2. What is the central theme of these poems?
3. List any quotations that have come into general usage in our speech.
4. From what aspects of life did he draw his figures of speech?
5. Do these prophecies contain more or less reflection on the present situation of the people than one finds in the eighth-century prophets?

v

Jeremiah 1:4-19; 12:1-6; 15:10-12; 15:15-21; 20:7-13; 20:14-18.

1. What was the basis of Jeremiah's struggle?
2. Compare these laments with Psalm 69. What may have been the origin of the lament form that Jeremiah uses?
3. Did Jeremiah experience God's sympathy?

vi

Jeremiah 31:1-40 (note verses 27-34).

1. What was Jeremiah's hope for the future?
2. Was it limited to Judah?
3. Did Jeremiah think of the new covenant as effective in his day?
4. Would the new covenant be based on a new book of law, replacing the law found by Josiah? Why?
5. Would the new covenant be between the nation and Yahweh? Why?

Read one of the following:

Anderson, *Understanding the Old Testament,* pp. 300-305 and 326-356.

Bewer and Kraeling, *Literature of the Old Testament,* pp. 153-181.

Buber, *The Prophetic Faith,* pp. 158-183.

Gottwald, *A Light to the Nations,* pp. 352-371.

Ezekiel

Ezekiel (ca. 593-571 B.C.), like Jeremiah, was a priest; unlike Jeremiah he showed great interest in the ritual side of religion. He was apparently exiled to Babylonia in 598 and there had his vision of God, which demonstrated to him conclusively what had been implicit in earlier prophetic teaching, that the people and the prophet could directly encounter Yahweh even in the land of exile. (See the historical outline, p. 40.)

Ezekiel's earlier prophecies are predictions of destruction for the nation. Though living in exile, he spoke at first not to the exiles, but to the people of Judah. (Some scholars have maintained that he was actually in Jerusalem for part of this time, but this is not stated in the book.) The sins of which he accused Judah included social injustice and also, with great emphasis, idolatry and disobedience to the ceremonial commands. Right ritual was important to Ezekiel because it was the way to honor God's holiness and majesty. Neglect of ritual worship meant treating Yahweh carelessly.

After the destruction of Jerusalem by Nebuchadnezzar in 587 B.C., Ezekiel's prophecies took a different form. He spoke to the exiles, and his message to them was one of comfort and hope. His prophecies of hope were worked out along two lines. First he urged on the exiles their individual responsibility. They were very much discouraged. They had been deported; their nation had been destroyed; they felt that they were overwhelmed by the collective ruin of their group. Against their discouragement Ezekiel preached their individual responsibility and God's concern for them as individuals. He also stressed the importance of the present. Their past history was bad, but if they changed their ways, God would forget their past. When he spoke of individual rewards and punishments, Ezekiel was speaking entirely in terms of the present life. In Judaism his view of reward for individual righteousness became the prevailing one for several centuries; a similar point of view (developed independently) is found in Proverbs.

Ezekiel's other line of thought that showed hope for the future dealt with the community. He held that God, for the sake of His own honor, would restore Jerusalem. Ezekiel's picture of the restored Jerusalem stressed ritual and ceremony. One purpose of the elaborate forms of worship was to emphasize the difference between the Jew and the outsider. Thus his hope for the future was for the chosen people only. This narrowness was in part dictated by the circumstances of the time. The tiny, discouraged group of worshippers of Yahweh needed to be separated from the surrounding world, or else they would be swallowed up in their environment. Ezekiel's emphasis on the separateness of the chosen people and his stress on religious, rather than national bonds of community were both very influential and have earned for him the name "the father of Judaism."

Readings

i

Ezekiel 1:1-3:21.

1. What was Ezekiel's occupation before the exile?
2. Where was he when he had his vision?
3. See II Kings 24:14-17 on how he got there.
4. What does this vision imply as to where one can worship Yahweh?
5. Compare Ezekiel's understanding of his task with that of earlier prophets.

ii

Ezekiel 8:1-18; 12:1-20; 14:12-23; 15:1-8; 22:23-31; 24:15-27; 33:21-33.

1. What was Ezekiel's idea of Jerusalem's future?
2. Of what sins did he accuse Jerusalem?
3. Did he emphasize ritualistic or social sins?
4. Were these passages written before or after the fall of Jerusalem?
5. Compare the form of Ezekiel's message with that of the earlier prophets.

iii

Ezekiel 20:1-44.

1. How did Ezekiel understand the people's beginnings? Compare with Amos 5:25, Hosea 11:1-4, and Jeremiah 7:21-23.
2. What had saved the people up to Ezekiel's time?
3. What lay immediately ahead? Why?

iv

Ezekiel 11:13-21; 36:22-36; 37:1-14.

1. What was the basis for hope in these prophecies?
2. Compare Ezekiel 36:22-36 with Jeremiah 31:27-34. What likenesses and differences do you see in the pictures of the future?
3. What aspect of God is most clearly apparent in the prophecies of Ezekiel?

v

Ezekiel 18:1-32.

1. How did Ezekiel modify the older understanding of the people's relationship to Yahweh?
2. Why was the new basis presented in this passage a practical necessity?
3. Study the tests for righteousness in this chapter. What sorts of acts are most prominent?
4. Is the external act or the intention toward Yahweh more important to Ezekiel?

vi

Ezekiel 40:1-43:5.

1. What is the primary concern in this vision of a restored Jerusalem?

2. Did this section arise more directly out of the prophetic or the priestly tradition?
3. Could Judaism have come through the exile without Ezekiel's emphasis on ceremonial purity?

Read one of the following:

Anderson, *Understanding the Old Testament,* pp. 359-375.

Bewer and Kraeling, *Literature of the Old Testament,* pp. 182-199.

Buber, *The Prophetic Faith,* pp. 183-188.

Gottwald, *A Light to the Nations,* pp. 380-398.

Second Isaiah

Chapters 40-66 of the book of Isaiah are very different from Chapters 1-39. In the earlier chapters Isaiah is mentioned by name; there are frequent historical or biographical sections; the circumstances are those of the eighth century B.C.: Ahaz and Hezekiah are the kings; Jerusalem is threatened by Assyria. In Chapters 40-66 Isaiah is never mentioned; there are no historical or biographical sections; the circumstances are those of the sixth century B.C.: the Hebrews are in exile; the Babylonians and Persians are the great powers. (See the historical outline, p. 40.) The best explanation of such facts is that the later section was written by an unknown prophet during the exile, whom we label "Second Isaiah." We limit our study to Chapters 40-55, since Chapters 56-66 may come from a somewhat later date and from another prophet or prophets.

Second Isaiah, like Ezekiel, confronted the discouragement of the exile, but he did so in a very different way. The individualism of reward and punishment that we find in Ezekiel is lacking in Second Isaiah. This prophet proclaimed the goodness of God in choosing Israel in a way that helped give meaning to the experience of the exile.

He believed that the community rightly had to suffer for its sins; he said that their suffering exceeded the proportion due them; and he held that the period of suffering was nearly completed. Though the people thought that they were forgotten by God, the prophet held before them the hope of a bright future. God is good—the unfailing, loyal love of God for His people is the most real thing in the

world. Therefore Second Isaiah could have only hope for the future;
he painted glowing, poetic pictures of the return from exile and
rebuilding of Jerusalem; and encouragement was his constant message.

On the other hand, the universal rule of God was far more clearly
expressed by Second Isaiah than by any earlier prophet. God ruled
all nature, all history, all nations—earlier prophets had said this,
or nearly said it, but they did not reflect about it as Second Isaiah
did. From these assertions he drew the conclusion: the other gods
are simply nothing. They are unreal, and their idols are silly delu-
sions. In other words, Second Isaiah's universalism did not mean
that he tried to see good in other religions. Quite the opposite: the
God and the religion of a tiny, forgotten, exiled people are the only
real God and the only real religion.

Second Isaiah went even further. Yahweh not only ruled all nations; He also cared for them. God's purpose was that all people
should know Him.

God's redemptive purpose for the nations and the sufferings of
His people were brought into closest relation in the "servant poems"
(Sections vi and vii of the readings). Israel was God's servant, suffering in exile until God was ready to provide a return in glory. The
return would show God's power to the nations; but God's love could
be shown by the way in which His people, as they bore their sufferings, had the same spirit that God has. Thus the other nations
would see that Yahweh is the only God, and the sufferings of Israel
would play a part in God's work of saving the world.

The servant poems bring together themes drawn from the covenant tradition, themes from the calling and work of the prophets,
and themes from the sacrificial worship. The servant is presented as
one called by God, appointed to speak for God, and made a "vicari-
ous sacrifice" or offering for the sake of others. Israel's suffering was
not only for its own sins, but was also on behalf of other nations,
which God also loved.

The prophet spoke of Israel as God's servant, but in the servant
poems themselves the imagery is largely that of an individual person
as servant. The modern reader probably makes more of this distinction than the prophet himself did, for he thought of individual and
community as each finding their existence in the other. He believed
that the future would bring a deliverance that would extend to all

nations and that God would use Israel, even the defeated and suffering Israel, for this high purpose.

Readings

i

Isaiah 39:1-8; 40:1-5.

1. Describe the changes in style and message that occur with the beginning of Chapter 40.

ii

Isaiah (a) *40:1, 2; 41:5, 8-20;* (b) *40:3-5; 40:9-11;* (c) *40:6-8; 40:21-31;* (d) *40:12-17; 41:1-4;* (e) *40:18-20; 41:6-7* [1]*; 41:21-29.*

1. State the main theme in each of these groups of passages.
2. List passages in Chapters 42-45 that have the same themes and so can be listed with group *a, b, c, d,* or *e.*
3. Are there any passages in these chapters that do not fit into any of these groups?
4. What was Second Isaiah's view of the past? Of the present and future?
5. How much of history was meaningful to him? How did he relate his view of history to his view of God's character?

iii

Isaiah 44:24-45:7; 41:1; 46:8-11.

1. What evidence of date do you find in these passages?

iv

Isaiah 42:5-9; 45:5-8, 18-23; 46:5-11; 49:1-6.

1. How do these passages present the relation of Yahweh to foreign nations? Israel's relation to these nations? Compare them with the earlier prophets.
2. What similarity do you see between these passages and Genesis 1?

[1] In the Smith-Goodspeed translation, these verses follow 40:19.

v

Isaiah 41:8-10; 44:1-5, 21-22; 45:4; 49:3-5.

1. Who is the servant of Yahweh in these passages?

vi

Isaiah 42:1-4; 49:1-6; 50:4-9.

1. To what purpose is the servant dedicated?
2. How will this purpose be accomplished?

vii

Isaiah 52:13-53:12.

1. Who is the servant in this passage?
2. Who is speaking in 53:1-9?
3. Do the passages in Sections vi and vii present the same servant as the passages in Section v?

Read one of the following:

Anderson, *Understanding the Old Testament,* pp. 399-429.

Bewer and Kraeling, *Literature of the Old Testament,* pp. 214-228.

Buber, *The Prophetic Faith,* pp. 202-235.

Gottwald, *A Light to the Nations,* pp. 399-426.

Other Prophets

I—Eighth Century.

MICAH (ca. 735 B.C., a rural contemporary of Isaiah.)
Read the book of Micah.

Micah 1:1-3:12.

1. List passages that parallel other eighth-century prophets.
2. Compare with Isaiah's view of the future Jerusalem.

Micah 4:1-5.

3. Compare with Isaiah 2:2-4.

Micah 6:6-8.

4. This is probably the best-known passage in the writings of the eighth-century prophets. Note how neatly it summarizes the messages of the other three prophets of this century.

II—Seventh Century.

ZEPHANIAH (late seventh century B.C., a contemporary of Jeremiah; Zephaniah was a citizen of Jerusalem and perhaps an aristocrat.)
Read the book of Zephaniah.

Zephaniah 1:1-2:7.

1. What was Zephaniah's reaction to the condition of Judah?

Zephaniah 3:1-7.

2. What sins of Judah convinced him that she was worthy of destruction?

NAHUM (ca. 612 B.C.; unlike his predecessors, Nahum did not describe the doom of the Hebrews, but that of the great enemy, the Assyrians. Nineveh, the Assyrian capital, fell to the Babylonians and Medes in 612 B.C.)
Read the book of Nahum.

Nahum 1:2-10.

1. Compare Nahum's concept of Yahweh with that of other prophets.

Nahum 2:1-13.

2. Note the vivid imagery.

Nahum 3:1-19.

3. Why was Assyria destroyed? Did Nahum have anything to say about Judah's sins?

HABAKKUK (probably ca. 600 B.C.)
Read the book of Habakkuk.

Habakkuk 1:1-2:4.

1. To whom did Habakkuk address himself?
2. State the problem that troubled the prophet.

3. Was his problem an individual one or a problem of a corporate group?
4. What answer did Habakkuk find?

Habakkuk 2:5-20.

5. Compare with earlier prophetic statements about sin and punishment.

Habakkuk 3:1-19.

6. This psalm is probably not part of the original work. What is its theme?

Habakkuk 3:17-19.

7. Did the writer ask for a reward for goodness?

III—Sixth Century.

OBADIAH (sixth or fifth century; the occasion for the book seems to have been an Arabian invasion of Edom.)
Read the book of Obadiah.

Obadiah 1:1-20.

1. Edomites had occupied southern Judah after its destruction by Nebuchadnezzar. What was Obadiah's reaction to this act?
2. Contrast the spirit of Obadiah with that of the book of Lamentations.
3. Explain "your brother" in verse 12.
4. What was Obadiah's view of the outcome?

HAGGAI (about 520 B.C., in the restored Jerusalem.)
Read the book of Haggai.

Haggai 1:1-15; 2:10-23.

1. Compare Haggai's attitude toward ritual with that of the pre-exilic prophets.
2. What did the prophet promise if the Temple were rebuilt?
3. What political hopes did the prophet have?

ZECHARIAH (about 520 B.C., in the restored Jerusalem.)
Read the book of Zechariah.

Zechariah 1:7-17.

1. Note the form of the prophecy. Does it resemble that of any earlier prophets?
2. In what way did the nations disobey Yahweh?
3. What was Yahweh's promise?

Zechariah 4:6-10.

4. Zerubbabel was a descendant of David. Compare with the political hope of Haggai.

Zechariah 8:1-23.

5. How successfully had Jerusalem been rebuilt?
6. What was the writer's attitude toward foreign nations? What earlier prophet did he resemble in this?
7. See note about Zechariah 9-14 on page 107.

IV—Fifth and Fourth Century.

MALACHI (perhaps ca. 460 B.C., a collection of anonymous prophecies.)
Read the book of Malachi.

Malachi 1:6-14.

1. In what ways would this prophecy fit well the time just before Nehemiah's reform? (See Nehemiah 13.)

Malachi 2:10-16.

2. What gave this prophet the clearest evidence that the social life of the people was not in accord with the covenant?

Malachi 3:7-10.

3. What should the people do to gain God's blessing?
4. Compare Malachi with the pre-exilic prophets.

JOEL (probably fourth century; Joel could well be grouped with the apocalyptic rather than with the prophetic books.)
Read the book of Joel.

Joel 2:28-3:21.

1. What results from the possession of God's spirit?
2. What sort of concept of God is implied?

3. Who is judged and on what basis?
4. Compare 3:9-10 with Isaiah 2:4.

JONAH (probably fourth century; not a prophetic book at all, but a story about a prophet.)
Read the book of Jonah.

1. State the message of this book in your own words.
2. Where else has it appeared in the Old Testament?

6

The Legal Literature

The major literary work of the priests is the Torah, the fivefold book of law or Pentateuch—Genesis through Deuteronomy. This great work—the core of the Old Testament—arose in the context of worship. The narratives were remembered in connection with the festivals that commemorated them (see Deuteronomy 26:1-11 and p. 22). Many of the laws dealt with the regulation of worship, others with the relation of man to man. All were understood equally as claims for obedience to Yahweh. The deliverance that God had worked in the past was made real in the present, and the claim of God for obedience regularly confronted the worshipper.

Moses was thought of as the great law-giver, and in New Testament times Torah was sometimes called "Moses" (Luke 16:29). Yet Moses' teachings grew and were interpreted through years of oral tradition. There seems to have been a written code of law as early as Solomon's time—the Book of the Covenant (Exodus 20:23-23:19). But the completed written Torah did not become a determining force in the Hebrew community until post-exilic times, when it became the constitution of the Jewish community in Palestine.

77

Running through the entire law is evidence of a striving to achieve a fixed form of national life based on tradition and authority, specifying in advance concrete patterns of behavior, guiding both moral and cultic obedience to God, and vigorously emphasizing the separation between Israel and other peoples. In the time of the divided monarchy, the priestly traditionalism stood in sharp tension with the more radical claim for obedience found in the prophets. As the priestly-legal movement gained strength in post-exilic times, it inherited and incorporated an impetus toward obedience from the fast-weakening prophetic movement. The obedience taught by the priests was less radical than that demanded by the prophets, but it bore the stamp of the prophets even in its more practical and legalistic form.

Deuteronomy

We shall discuss Deuteronomy, the fifth book of the Pentateuch, as a clear example of this tension between pure obedience and the practical. As early as the fourth century A.D., scholars suggested that Deuteronomy may have been the "book of law" discovered by Josiah and used as the basis for his reform (see p. 39). While it seems probable that the central portion of the book was Josiah's book of law, many scholars think that Deuteronomy did not find its present form until after the exile. Some see Deuteronomy as the introductory volume of the "Deuteronomistic history" running through Joshua, Judges, I and II Samuel, and I and II Kings.

However late the final form may be, most scholars hold that the original writing in the book is the work of the priests of the northern kingdom, beginning before and continuing after the fall of Samaria. The exact process by which the book received its present form is a continuing problem for scholars. The writing may have begun as a record to guide a recurring ceremony of covenant renewal. The emphasis on "love" and a number of oft-used phrases indicate a close relationship to Hosea and Jeremiah, both of whom were closely associated with the traditions of the northern kingdom. Several laws reflect the teachings of Amos, who preached in Israel.

Some elements in the book, such as the system of rewards and punishments (all located in this world), the emphasis on social and human values, and a persuasive appeal to reason reflect the kind of religious wisdom we find in parts of the book of Proverbs. These elements seem to come from a time of little tension, when the priests were comfortably and conservatively carrying out their duties at the shrines.

On the other hand, the major theme of the book comes from elements that seem to reflect times of tension, when Yahweh worship was under attack as it was in Israel under Jezebel in the ninth century and in Judah under Manasseh in the seventh. The urgent and repeated warnings against idols and false gods show the priests of Yahweh on the defensive. There can be little doubt that the central portion of the book (Chapters 5-26, 28)—probably Josiah's book of law—found its present form in a time of tension. Time and again the instruction about details of the law gives way to urgent exhortation to "hear, O Israel," to be "careful to obey," to be " a holy people to the Lord your God." The overwhelming piling up of curse on curse with which Chapter 28 closes brings this note of urgency to a deafening crescendo.

In form, the book of Deuteronomy is presented as a series of orations delivered by Moses near the end of his life, in which he reviews the laws of Yahweh. This form gives the book its name, Deuteronomy—literally, "second law." The constantly reiterated theme "Israel shall worship Yahweh only" is as old as Moses. The author or editor who gave the book its present form had a basic style and theology that gave unity not only to this book but also to the entire Deuteronomistic history that follows it.

Readings

i

Deuteronomy 12:1-32.

1. What is the main object of the laws in this passage?

   Exodus 20:22-26. I Samuel 1:19-28; 7:5-11; 21:1-7. Judges 11:11; 18:31.

2. Do these passages reflect familiarity with the instructions of Deuteronomy 12 in regard to place of worship? in regard to worship of idols?

Deuteronomy 12:20-25; 14:24-26; 18:6-8.

3. Do these passages seem to be answering practical questions raised by the changing of an established system? Describe the specific changes suggested by these passages and the reasons for them.

ii

Deuteronomy 6:14; 7:1-6, 25; 8:11-20 (note verses *17, 19*); *9:6-21; 11:28; 12:29-31; 13:1-3; 27:15.*

1. What is the constantly recurring theme found here?

iii

Deuteronomy 4:19; 17:3. II Kings 21:1-6. Jeremiah 7:16-20; 8:1-3. Zephaniah 1:5.

1. Note the "host of heaven" in the list of idols.
2. When was the "host" brought to Jerusalem?
3. Did the eighth-century prophets condemn idolatry? Did they mention idolatry? Did they mention the host of heaven?
4. Was the worship of the host of heaven a problem in the seventh century? (Jeremiah and Zephaniah began to preach in the late seventh century.)
5. What conclusion can you draw from this evidence as to the date of these verses in Deuteronomy?

Deuteronomy 17:8-13.

6. How would this law affect the status of the priesthood?

II Kings 22:1-23:30.

7. Did Josiah carry out the reform of Deuteronomy 12?
8. Note II Kings 23:9. Did Deuteronomy 18:6-8 prove adequate in actual practice?

iv

Deuteronomy 5:1-21.

1. Compare this with Exodus 20:1-17. Note especially the command about the Sabbath. What difference in point of view is reflected in the different forms of this commandment?

Deuteronomy 4:2, 13; 5:22; 12:32.

2. What place did the decalogue have in the law?

v

Deuteronomy 15:7-11; 24:10-22.

1. Compare the treatment of duty to the poor with that shown in the prophets.
2. Do these laws advocate the punishment of the individual or do they hold to the idea of collective guilt? Compare with Joshua 7:22-26.
3. What motive for kindness to the poor is mentioned?

vi

Deuteronomy 7:12-16; 11:13-15; 28:1-68.

1. What kind of action is urged here?
2. What kind of reward is promised?
3. Does the reward affect the individual or the group? Compare with Deuteronomy 24:16. How do you explain the difference?
4. Do you note any sections in Deuteronomy 28 that might come from a still later date than that of Josiah?

vii

Deuteronomy 4:25-31.

1. What event does this seem to describe?

Deuteronomy 4:39.

2. What relation do you see between this verse and Second Isaiah?

The books of Joshua, Judges, Samuel, and Kings probably come from the period immediately following Deuteronomy. Readings in these books are found in the historical outline (pp. 29, 34, 36, 39). To see the influence of Deuteronomy on their organization, read the following:

Judges 2:6-3:6; 4:1-6; 6:1-8; 10:6-16; 13:1.

1. State the theory of history found in the first passage.
2. How do the connecting links between the stories reflect this theory?
3. Do the links speak of a nation or of tribes?
4. Do the stories deal with a nation or with tribes?

viii

Deuteronomy 6:4-9; 7:6-11; 9:4-12; 10:12-11:32.

1. State the basic theme and theology of Deuteronomy as reflected in these passages.
2. Why did Yahweh choose Israel?

Read one of the following:

Anderson, *Understanding the Old Testament,* pp. 305-320.

Bewer and Kraeling, *Literature of the Old Testament,* pp. 125-143.

Gottwald, *A Light to the Nations,* pp. 334-346.

The Documentary Theory of the Authorship of the Pentateuch

When Josiah established the book of law found in the temple as the basis for the covenant with Yahweh and "all the people confirmed the covenant" (II Kings 23:3), a new conception of the importance of the written book began to emerge. Dating from this beginning, the worship of Yahweh gradually became the "religion of the Book." In one sense Josiah's reform was the birth of the Bible.

By the time the law had been established as authoritative Scripture in the fifth or fourth century B.C. (see Nehemiah 8:1-18), Deuteronomy was only part of a very much larger book. This book, known as the Torah (which we call the law), has since been divided into five books, the first five books of our Old Testament. Contained in these books are not only the basic legal literature of the Hebrews, but also their records of their history up to the period of the conquest.

Much of the serious study of the Pentateuch in the past century has centered in the question of its origin. Coming out of much discussion, the "Documentary Theory" of its origin has won wide acceptance. It is admittedly a theory, based entirely on internal evidence such as the duplications, contradictions, and changes in style and vocabulary found throughout. Also, continuing study is modifying the theory so that few informed scholars agree on all details. The theory is accepted in principle, however, by most Protestant scholars.

The theory holds that the first five books of the Old Testament are composed of a number of originally separate "documents," that these documents were composed at different times and places over a period of from four to five centuries, that some of the documents were primarily narrative and some primarily legal, and that eventually these documents were woven together into the book that was canonized as the Torah.

In its usual form the documentary theory has identified the separate sources of the Pentateuch as four in number: two of these were primarily narratives and two were collections of laws. The narrative documents, J and E as they are called, were combined to form a great history of the Hebrews into which the laws were later inserted by an editor who rounded out the whole. Current study emphasizes two things that are not brought out in the brief outline below: for one thing, the documents grew with time, rather than being written all at once; for another, even at late periods, really old tradition was incorporated into them.

Below is a sketch of the characteristics of the four "documents" and a table showing the distribution of the documents through the five books of the law.

A. Sketch of the documents of the documentary theory.

> *J document*—ca. 900 B.C.
> Uses Yahweh as name of God from the beginning.
> Probably orginated in Judah about 1000 B.C.; was revised and expanded around 900.
> A history beginning with creation.
> Informal, conversational style.
> Uncritical in regard to anthropomorphisms.
> Interested in the beginnings of things.
> *E document*—ca. 750-700 B.C.
> Uses Elohim (God) as name for God, to the story of Moses and the burning bush.
> Written in Israel (Ephraim).
> A history beginning with Abraham.
> More formal than J.
> Free from anthropomorphisms.
> More moralistic than J.
> *D document*—ca. 650 B.C.
> The core of Deuteronomy; the law found during Josiah's reform.
> *J-E* Combined into one story about 600 B.C. in Judah.
> *P document*—The work of priests covering a period of about a century before 450 B.C. and including:

(1) *A History*
   Very formal in style.
   Beginning with creation.
   Tells stories explaining the origin of religious practices.
(2) *A Collection of Laws*
   Carefully codified, though based on earlier laws.
   At points in advance of D's ethics.
   More concerned with ritual cleanliness and the rights of priests than D.
(3) *Genealogies and Chronologies*
   Carefully worked out, partly as a form of history and partly because of the priestly interest in racial purity.
   Used in tying the four documents together.
(4) *Editorial Work*
   Sometimes called R (Redactor).
   The editors combined all four documents to form a single law or Torah, which was later divided into the Pentateuch, or fivefold book.
   Since the J and E narratives extended into the conquest and therefore form sources for the present book of Joshua, the term Hexateuch (sixfold book) is sometimes used to denote the total collection that is the subject of the documentary theory.

B. Table of distribution of the documents through the books of law.

Genesis	Exodus	Leviticus	Numbers	Deuteronomy
J	J		J	
E	E		E	
				D
P	P	P	P	P

In the following readings, Sections i-ii point to some of the variety in the laws, which is evidence for holding that there are various sources for the law. Sections iii-v illustrate repetitions in the narratives that make probable the existence of various sources. The section on Genesis that follows is designed to indicate some of the leading religious ideas of Genesis. For the narrative content of Exodus and Numbers, see the historical outline.

Readings

i

Compare the following pairs of passages:

Deuteronomy 24:8 and Leviticus 13:1-14:57.
Exodus 33:7-11 and Exodus 25:1-27:21.
Deuteronomy 14 and Leviticus 11.

1. In each of these pairs, which passage shows a more advanced legalism?
2. Would the description of the tabernacle come from before or after Solomon's Temple? before or after Ezekiel 40-48?
3. Would a late date for Leviticus explain Jeremiah 7:21-23 and Amos 5:25?

ii

The following passages are listed in the order in which they appear in the Bible. List them in their proper chronological order. Explain the appearance of contradicting laws in the Pentateuch. Date the law in Leviticus.

Exodus 21:2-6   Deuteronomy 15:12-18
Leviticus 25:39-46   Jeremiah 34:8-22

iii

Read Genesis 1:1 through 3:24. Do you find one or two stories here? Is the order of creation the same in the first and second chapters? Is there any repetition? Is there a difference in style? Where is the dividing line?

iv

Read Genesis 12:10-20 and Genesis 20. How do you account for the repetition of this story? Which chapter uses the name "the Lord" (Yahweh) for God; which uses "God" (Elohim)? Which story is more moralistic?

v

Read the flood stories as separated in the Supplementary Materials, pp. 174-183. Answer the questions found there.

Read one of the following:

Anderson, *Understanding the Old Testament,* pp. 154-173.

Bewer and Kraeling, *Literature of the Old Testament,* Chap. 5-6, 9, 17.

Bright, *A History of Israel,* pp. 61-69.

Gottwald, *A Light to the Nations,* pp. 102-114.

The Interpreter's Bible, Vol. I, pp. 185-200.

Genesis

While the history of the Hebrews *as a nation* begins with the book of Exodus, the great book of Genesis contains the Hebrews' record of the beginning of things—up to their entrance into Egypt. The first eleven chapters tell the stories of creation, the flood, and the tower of Babel, along with genealogies from Adam to Abraham. These stories are not history, but expressions of faith in symbolic form—myths, as these are often called. They differ from the myths of the surrounding nations in that they do not directly present the foundation of man's relation to God, but lead forward to the encounter between God and His people that follows in the book of Exodus.

The story of Abraham begins with Chapter 12, and the remainder of the book is devoted to Abraham, Isaac, Jacob, and Joseph. Actually the stories of Abraham and Jacob hold the center of attention —Abraham who was called of God, and Jacob whose name was changed to Israel. Even the beautifully told story of Joseph does not take precedence over the record of Israel, whose children were the Hebrews. We call these stories legends because, while they come out of a concrete historical setting and often reflect real historical events, they were told and retold for many years before being written down, and are not concerned with exactness of historical recollection. Like the earlier stories, these chapters are written to present the faith, rather than to remember the facts of history.

The book illustrates throughout how the Hebrew mind interpreted all history in terms of Yahweh's plans and purposes. Particularly does it emphasize the conviction that Israel is Yahweh's chosen people—successful not because of her strength or her worth, but only because of Yahweh's choice.

The common reader, reading Genesis rapidly, his interest caught up in the story, comes to Exodus with an insight into the central themes of Old Testament faith. Without pondering an involved and abstract tome of theology, he has learned that:

1. There is one God, Creator of light and darkness, day and night, sun, moon, and stars, the waters above and beneath the earth, and every living thing upon the earth. None of these creatures is a god, for all of them are created by and under the control of the Lord God Almighty.

2. Man is a creature—made in "the image" of God (Genesis 1:26), given sovereignty over the earth and its other creatures, but himself a creature, not a god.

3. Man persistently seeks to usurp the place of God; he eats forbidden fruit; he will go to the extreme of murder in attempting to rule over his brother; and "every imagination of the thoughts of his heart is only evil continually" (Genesis 6:5).

4. The judgment of God is inevitable and universal. Man is driven from paradise, marked for life, wiped out by a flood, dispersed in confusion.

5. The will of God cannot be thwarted by man. Man continues to live through the mercy of God and is given an undeserved second chance.

6. God has chosen a people through whom He purposes to establish His will, with whose ancestors He had made a covenant, and to whom He will reveal His law.

A careful reading of Genesis also reveals the characteristics that have given rise to the documentary theory. The sudden changes in style, the duplications, the contradictions, the vocabulary differences all point to a variety of original sources. Illustrations are found in the readings on the documentary theory, Sections iii-v. (See above, p. 85.)

The following readings point to some of the central religious convictions of the book of Genesis.

Readings

i

Genesis 1:1-2:25.

1. What is the significance of the fact that the creation of the whole world is the work of the Hebrew God?

2. In a world familiar with stories of creation coming out of conflict between divine powers, what would be the impact of the creation stories of Genesis?
3. What is the relation of man to the rest of creation?
4. Note Isaiah 45:5-8. Do you see a parallel between Second Isaiah and the priestly account of creation?

ii

Genesis 3:1-24; 6:5-9:17; 11:1-9.

1. In what way do these narratives prepare the way for the covenant with Abraham?

iii

Genesis 1:28-30; 9:1-7; 12:1-3; 13:14-17; 15:5-7; 26:2-5; 26:23-24; 28:10-19; 35:9-12; 50:24.

1. Note how "covenant" runs throughout the book.
2. What new note appears in the covenant with Abraham?
3. Did any of these men seek Yahweh, or did He choose them?

iv

Genesis 45:1-13; 46:1-4.

1. How did Joseph explain his being sold as a slave by his brothers?
2. Why did Jacob go to Egypt?
3. Do you think the authors of Genesis saw any parallel between the story of Joseph and Israel's history?

Read one of the following:

Anderson, *Understanding the Old Testament,* pp. 173-182.

Gottwald, *A Light to the Nations,* pp. 448-465.

The Interpreter's Bible, Vol. I, pp. 439-457, esp. pp. 453-56.

Wright and Fuller, *The Book of the Acts of God,* pp. 47-73.

7

The Wisdom Literature

The wisdom literature in the Old Testament consists of the books of Proverbs, Job, and Ecclesiastes, and some of the Psalms (for instance, Psalms 1, 37, 49, 128). These books present a striking contrast to most of the rest of the Old Testament. The law, the prophets, and the histories all are concerned with the story of one continuing group of people and God's dealings with that group. But in the wisdom books the Hebrew community as such is ignored—along with the exodus and covenant, the history of the Hebrews, the prophets, the heroes of the past, and, for the most part, the law. In other words, the authors of the wisdom books did not make use of the assumption of most of the Old Testament that God is uniquely known in His relation to a special people. The wisdom books deal with man, not with the Hebrews. Furthermore, they deal with man as an individual, though the individual's life is seen in its relation with friend and enemy, family and neighborhood, work, and the like. The wisdom writers were interested in common sense; they believed in studying life and seeing what kinds of results followed various sorts of action. Many of their proverbs say nothing about God, and it is quite possible that in its origin the wisdom movement was purely practical—the study of how to get ahead in the world. As we know them now, however, the wisdom books are religious. They look for the work of God in the events of daily life.

The wisdom movement was not limited to the Hebrews. Similar writings came from Egypt and Babylonia. Hebrew sages learned and borrowed from these sources; they were in fact part of a movement that was many centuries older than the Hebrew wisdom books we now possess. The Old Testament wisdom writings, however, are all relatively late. They are hard to date, because they are not interested in history and do not reflect contemporary events. In their present form, however, they all date from the post-exilic period. They are a reminder that the law and the Temple were not the only interests of religious Jews in the centuries that followed Ezra and Nehemiah. One must remember as well that the wisdom tradition has a long history among the Hebrews, even though our knowledge of pre-exilic wisdom is limited.

The Book of Proverbs

Solomon is said to have been the first great Hebrew collector of proverbs (I Kings 4:29-34). However, the book of Proverbs as we know it is much later than Solomon. It is an anthology drawn from various sources, some of which are apparently not Hebrew (see the headings above Proverbs 30:1; 31:1). The date of the final collection is hard to fix. It falls in the post-exilic period, sometime after 400 B.C.

Proverbs is primarily a series of collections of short, pithy observations about success and failure, right and wrong, wisdom and foolishness. The sayings praise the commonsense virtues that make it easy for men to live together, and they state that the individuals who practice these virtues will be rewarded by long life, friends, influence, peace, and security. The wicked or foolish man will correspondingly suffer the loss of these good things. The religious assumption behind this point of view is that God can be known by studying His way of controlling the world. The book of Proverbs is confident that God is just, for the rewards and punishments men receive manifest His way of working. Little or nothing, however, is

said of God's mercy, and the book takes a rather hard-hearted attitude toward the wicked and the fools.

In the first nine chapters of the book of Proverbs there are a number of poems in praise of wisdom. Here wisdom is pictured poet-
ically as a woman making an appeal that men listen and learn from
her. The poems represent wisdom as the force or principle in accord
with which the world was created, and thus they represent a later,
more reflective type of thinking than is found in the rest of the
book.

Readings

i

Proverbs 10:1-14:35.

1. What do the wise men have to say about relations with friends?
   about women and marriage? education and children? work?
2. How do they advise getting along with a fool?
3. What interest do they show in ritual?
4. Compare the ethic presented here with that of the Ten Commandments.
5. Compare the concept of righteousness presented here with that
   of Second Isaiah.

ii

Proverbs 2:1-3:35.

1. What is the reward of wisdom? When does it occur?
2. What is the opposite of wisdom?
3. Does the code of wisdom apply to social problems or to individual living?

iii

Proverbs 30:1-33.

1. Compare the form of these poems with the section read above.
2. Read verses 1-4. How do they differ in spirit from the rest of the
   book?

iv

Proverbs 1:1-33; 8:1-36; 9:1-6, 13-18. Job 28:1-28.

1. Notice how wisdom is personified or objectified. How literally was this personification meant to be taken?
2. Notice the relation of wisdom to the creation.
3. According to the wisdom teachers, how is God known? How does this differ from the prophets' view?
4. Is there any difference between the attitude toward the fool in these sections and that seen in section i of these readings?

Read one of the following:

Anderson, *Understanding the Old Testament,* pp. 464-477.

Bewer and Kraeling, *Literature of the Old Testament,* pp. 321-329.

Gottwald, *A Light to the Nations,* pp. 463-472.

Ecclesiastes

The book of Ecclesiastes protests against the kind of teaching found in Proverbs. The writer, an anonymous wisdom teacher of the post-exilic period, writes as if he were Solomon, but his doing so is an obvious literary device. Koheleth (his name in Ecclesiastes 1:1, 12) had studied the same tradition that we find in the book of Proverbs. His rigorous testing found that tradition inadequate. The world, to him, does not reveal God's way of working, and God becomes an unknown quantity. Koheleth does not doubt God's existence, but it seems to him that God is capricious or even unfriendly. It is worth noticing that he refuses to look to the Hebrew tradition of the law and prophets to find a clue to God's will. Nevertheless he clings to the standards of a gentleman: in a dark and uncertain world moderation and self-control are the best hopes for some fleeting peace.

Some parts of the book express a more "orthodox" faith that God will bring men to judgment. Some of these sayings are probably the work of later editors.

Readings

i

Ecclesiastes 1:12-2:26; 3:9-5:9; 8:10-9:6.

1. Notice the author's method of investigation in 1:12-2:12.
2. List the supposedly good things of life that Koheleth has found futile.
3. Does he find anything good? If so, what?
4. What is his view on life after death?
5. Has this view appeared before?

ii

Ecclesiastes 1:1-11; 3:1-8; 5:10-20; 9:7-10:3; 11:9-12:8.

1. Does the philosophy of these poems vary from that of the prose essays above?
2. Notice the recurring figure of the circle in the first poem. How does this contrast with the presupposition of Hebrew religion that the continuing history of the community had meaning?
3. To whom is the last poem addressed?
4. What does it advise?
5. Does it read more smoothly with lines 4, 7, and 8 omitted? Can you account for this?

iii

1. On what grounds does the book of Ecclesiastes challenge the wisdom tradition as it is expressed in the book of Proverbs?

Read one of the following:

Anderson, *Understanding the Old Testament,* pp. 477-484.

Bewer and Kraeling, *Literature of the Old Testament,* pp. 344-354.

Gottwald, *A Light to the Nations,* pp. 486-490.

The Book of Job

The book of Job stands alone as a literary work. It is a poetic dialogue on the theme of finding God in the midst of tragedy and suffering. The core of the book is a discussion or debate between

Job, a righteous sufferer, and his friends about the meaning of Job's suffering. This discussion is concluded by God's address to Job. The poetic section is set in the framework of a prose story that explains how Job came to suffer and provides a happy ending not at all essential to the view set forth in the poems. The author (or authors) of the poems presents his own point of view in the speeches of Job and in the concluding speeches of God. The friends of Job are spokesmen for the conventional doctrine that individual goodness is visibly rewarded.

The book as we have it now is the work of more than one author. The poet of the dialogue has set his work in the framework of an older story about a righteous sufferer. The speeches of Elihu (Chapters 32-37) break the context and are probably a later addition, as some of the other poems may be. It is difficult to fix the date of the poems. Some scholars hold that they come from early in the exile; others would date them about 400 B.C.

Job stands in the wisdom tradition. The problem of Job is understood as his individual problem. No reference is made to the prophetic tradition; for instance, there is no hint of the approach to suffering found in Second Isaiah. Yet like Ecclesiastes, Job represents a vigorous protest against the view of life set forth in Proverbs. Unlike Ecclesiastes, the tone of Job's protest is religious. The disasters that have overtaken him destroy his faith in the accepted view of God's righteousness. He finds that suffering is not necessarily punishment, for he knows that his own suffering does not result from any wicked thing that he has done. In the face of his friends' attempt to support the old doctrine (which means, of course, blaming Job for some sort of sin), Job stormily maintains his innocence. His suffering has made God a mystery, and he desperately seeks to find God and to discover some meaning in his disaster. The violence and bitterness of his complaint, however, do not mean that he gives up the struggle. He believes that God is worth seeking, for from God's point of view there is some meaning in what happens to him.

The speeches of the Lord from the whirlwind do not tell Job why he suffers. These great rhetorical questions are usually interpreted in the light of one of two insights: (1) God the Creator is so holy, so far beyond the comprehension of any creature, that Job's demand to understand his plight is sinful impertinence, or (2) high and holy as God the Creator is, He is still compassionate enough to confront a lone, suffering creature and call him back to the true relationship of obedient faith. Probably both of these insights are necessary for a comprehension of the message of the book. However we interpret these speeches, it is clear that, in contrast to Ecclesiastes, the book of Job expresses both a deep conviction that man can find the presence of God even in the dark mystery of suffering and a faith that, impossible as it is for man to comprehend the transcendent God, there can be no question of His justice.

Readings

i

THE PROSE PROLOGUE, WHICH GIVES THE SETTING.

Job 1:1-2:13.

1. Is Job living in accord with the code of wisdom?
2. Why is he stricken?
3. Does the story so far raise the question "Why do the righteous suffer?"

ii

JOB'S PROTEST AND THE FIRST CYCLE OF DISCUSSION BETWEEN JOB AND HIS FRIENDS.

Job 3:1-14:22. Outline: Job's protest, Job 3. First speech of Eliphaz, Job 4-5. Job's reply, Job 6-7. First speech of Bildad, Job 8. Job's reply, Job 9-10. First speech of Zophar, Job 11. Job's reply, Job 12-14.

1. What is Job's complaint?
2. How do his friends explain what has happened to him?
3. Do their explanations differ?
4. Do they differ in their personal attitude toward Job?
5. Where does Job lay the blame for his fate?
6. In what spirit does he accept his fate?

iii

THE SECOND CYCLE OF DISCUSSION.

Job 15:1-21:34. Outline: Second speech of Eliphaz, Job 15. Job's reply, Job 16-17. Second speech of Bildad, Job 18. Job's reply, Job 19. Second speech of Zophar, Job 20. Job's reply, Job 21.

THE THIRD CYCLE OF DISCUSSION. (NOTICE THAT THE THIRD CYCLE IS
INCOMPLETE; APPARENTLY PART OF THIS CYCLE HAS DROPPED OUT, AND
SOME OF IT MAY NOW BE GIVEN TO THE WRONG SPEAKER.)

*Job 22:1-27:23. Outline: Third speech of Eliphaz, Job 22. Job's
reply, Job 23-24. Third speech of Bildad, Job 25. Job's reply, Job
26-27. (Part of Chapter 27 may be the missing speech of Zophar.)*

JOB'S FINAL SPEECH.

Job 29:1-31:40.

1. Are the friends less, or more, severe with Job as the discussion
   progresses?
2. Is Job less, or more, ready to admit his guilt?
3. Is he less, or more, interested in finding God?
4. Notice the following passages: Job 9:30-35; 14:13-22; 16:18-22;
   19:21-29; 23:1-17; 31:35-37. Is Job more interested in understanding his suffering or in finding God?
5. In the above passages (Question 4), does Job suggest any possible
   ways of meeting God beyond his present experience? What is his
   final answer to these possibilities?
6. In the book of Job, what are the standards of a good life? Compare with the book of Proverbs, Second Isaiah, and the Ten
   Commandments.

iv

A POEM IN PRAISE OF WISDOM.

Job 28.

1. Compare with Section iv of the readings in the book of Proverbs
   (see p. 92).

v

THE SPEECHES OF ELIHU.

Job 32:1-37:24.

1. What is Elihu's solution to the problem? Is it different from that
   of the three friends?

vi

THE VOICE FROM THE WHIRLWIND.

Job 38:1-41:34.

1. Does God explain Job's suffering? Does He explain His own justice?
2. State in your own words the answer that the voice gives.
3. What is the importance of the fact that God speaks to Job and not to the friends?

vii

JOB'S REPENTANCE AND THE EPILOGUE.

Job 42:1-16.

1. Of what does Job repent?
2. Is the prose epilogue orthodox or radical from the standpoint of the creed of wisdom?

viii

1. On what ground does the book of Job challenge the doctrine of wisdom?
2. What does it offer in place of that doctrine?

Read one of the following:

Anderson, *Understanding the Old Testament,* pp. 484-497.

Bewer and Kraeling, *Literature of the Old Testament,* pp. 329-344.

Gottwald, *A Light to the Nations,* pp. 472-486.

8

The Psalms

The book of Psalms was the hymnbook of the Temple in the post-exilic period. The psalms present the great variety of Hebrew worship and have no doubt been, in the church, the most used part of the Old Testament because of their profound expression of worship—the attitude and response of man before God. Probably the community was in the thought of the poets more often than the modern reader realizes, but in this collection both community and individual speak of their needs and of their thanksgiving to God. The prophetic faith in justice and the wisdom view of reward, the fierce patriotism of the nation and the despair of the individual, the boast of righteousness and the earnest plea for forgiveness all find voice in the psalms. For all their variety, they view life in its various aspects as lived under God; its meaning and value are sought in His purpose. Many of the psalms are pre-exilic in date; others come from late in the post-exilic period. All have been adapted for use in the various phases of worship in the Temple. The relation of some psalms to the particular form of worship in which they were used can still be seen, as this classification (based on that of Leslie, *The Psalms Translated and Interpreted in the Light of Hebrew Life and Worship*) shows.

Readings

PSALMS OF THE TEMPLE AND HOLY CITY

Psalm 46.

1. What city is the writer speaking of?
2. What prophet's teaching does the psalm resemble?

Psalm 84.

3. What does the writer find in the Temple? Compare with the prophets.

PSALMS OF PLEA FOR RESTORATION OF GOD'S PEOPLE

Psalms 123; 126.

1. What situation do these psalms reflect?

PSALMS FOR AND CONCERNING THE KING

Psalms 2; 110.

1. What will give security to the king? What does God promise to the king?
2. What is the relation of God to the king? to the nations of the world?

PSALMS OF GOD AS KING

Psalm 47.

1. Probably this (and other) psalms of God as King were used in a ceremonial procession that dramatized the enthronement of God. If so, what verses refer to the ceremony?
2. What is the writer's attitude toward foreign nations?

Psalm 93.

3. What is the power in comparison with which God's supreme power is shown? Compare with Psalms 74:12-15 and 89:9-10.

Psalm 96.

4. What is the writer's view of other gods?
5. What acts of God as King does the writer mention?

PSALMS OF REVELATION

Psalm 8.

1. Which is the more wonderful, nature or man?
2. What is the relation of God to nature? to man?

Psalm 104.

3. What aspect of natural processes does the writer emphasize?
4. Note the features of Palestine's natural life that he mentions.

Psalm 104:19-23.

5. Compare with the Hymn to the Sun of Amenhotep IV (Ikhnaton, 1375-58 B.C.):[1]

"When thou goest down in the western horizon,
The earth is in darkness as if it were dead.
Every lion cometh forth from his den,
And all snakes that bite.
When it is dawn, and thou risest in the horizon and shinest as
    the sun, it is day;
Thou dispellest the darkness and sheddest thy beams. . . .
The whole land doeth its work."

6. How is the thought of the Hebrew writer like that of the Egyptian? How is it different?
7. Which part of the psalm deals with the present? Which with the past?
8. What relation between man and God does it set forth?

Psalm 19:1-6.

9. How is God revealed in these verses? What characteristics of God are revealed?

Psalm 19:7-14.

10. How is God revealed in these verses? What characteristics of God are revealed?

Psalm 119.

11. An acrostic (alphabetic) psalm.[2]
12. How is God revealed in this psalm?
13. What is the writer's attitude toward the Law?

---

[1] Reprinted from Elmer A. Leslie, *The Psalms* (copyright 1949) by permission of the Abingdon Press.

[2] This and a number of other psalms are written with successive lines or groups of lines beginning with successive letters of the alphabet.

14. Does the writer find lovers of the Law in a majority or in a minority?

Psalm 78.

15. How is God revealed according to the author of this psalm?
16. How is this psalm like the teaching of the prophets?
17. How far does the writer carry his story?

PSALM LITURGIES

Psalm 24:1-6.

1. Who is about to enter the sanctuary in these verses? Compare the requirements for entry with Psalm 15.

Psalm 24:7-10.

2. Who is entering the sanctuary in these verses? What picture of God is presented here?

Psalm 100.

3. At what stage in a service of worship would this psalm be appropriate?
4. What picture of God is presented?

PSALMS OF THANKSGIVING AND CONFIDENCE

Psalm 65.

1. How is God related to nature?

Psalm 67.

2. At what season of the year was this psalm used?
3. What is this psalm's view of the relation between God and the nations of the earth?

Psalm 103.

4. What characteristic of God most impresses this psalmist?

Psalm 145.

5. This psalm is an acrostic (alphabetic) psalm. What is its theme?

Psalm 91.

6. What is the writer's conception of reward? Analyze the metaphors with which the reward is described. How literally did the writer mean these to be taken?

7. What is the attitude of the psalm toward the wicked?
8. Who speaks in verses 14-16?

Psalm 23.

9. Compare the theme of this psalm with that of Psalms 65 and 145.
10. What two metaphors are used for God?

Psalm 30.

11. For what specific benefit does this psalm give thanks?
12. What is the writer's attitude toward death?

Psalm 139.

13. What interest does this writer show in the national community?
14. What is the relation between God and the individual?

LAMENTS AND PRAYERS OF MEN IN DIFFICULTY

Psalm 58.

1. What understanding of God does this psalm present?
2. What is the writer's prayer?

Psalm 60.

3. State the subject of this lament.

Psalm 90.

4. What is the subject of this lament?
5. What importance does the psalm give to the individual? to the group?
6. What conception of God does the psalm present?

Psalm 7.

7. What is the writer's claim in verses 3-5?
8. Does the writer come to God with repentance?

Psalms 25; 26.

9. Compare these psalms. On what grounds does the writer of Psalm 25 appeal to God? Of Psalm 26?

Psalm 69.

10. What two problems does the writer face?
11. Does he claim to be without sin?

12. What is his attitude toward the charges made against him?
13. What is his attitude toward his enemies?

Psalm 39.

14. What relation does the writer assume between sickness and guilt?
15. What is his view of death?
16. What hope is there in human resources?
17. What does he believe God will do for him?

Psalm 88.

18. Compare with Psalm 39.
19. What argument does the poet offer God as a reason for granting him health?

PRAYERS OF THE PENITENT

Psalm 51.

1. What is the writer's conception of sin?
2. What is his conception of God?
3. What hope does he have for a good life?
4. What is his vow?
5. What is his attitude toward ritual? Are verses 18-19 consistent with verses 16-17?

Psalm 130.

6. What causes the separation between God and man?
7. How is it to be overcome?

WISDOM PSALMS

Psalm 37.

1. This is an acrostic (alphabetic) psalm.
2. What is the view of reward in this psalm?
3. How does the author reconcile himself to the prosperity of the wicked?

Psalm 73.

4. Compare the teaching on reward in this psalm with that in Psalm 37. Is it different? Is the author sure of himself?
5. Note verses 25-28. What view of reward is stated here?

Psalm 1.

6. Note the two types of men.
7. What does the psalm promise to the righteous?

Read one of the following:

Anderson, *Understanding the Old Testament,* pp. 444-445.

Bewer and Kraeling, *Literature of the Old Testament,* pp. 359-412.

Gottwald, *A Light to the Nations,* pp. 503-514.

9

Apocalyptic Literature: The Book of Daniel

pocalyptic literature represents both a continuation of and a change in the prophetic tradition. Its best example in the Old Testament is the book of Daniel. Only a few prophets had appeared in the post-exilic period, partly because men looked to the law to find God's will and partly because for a long time no crisis forced the Jews to a radical re-examination of their way of life. But the persecution of the second century B.C. shook the confidence of the Jews and stimulated a renewal of prophecy. The book of Daniel was written during this period of persecution, for it shows clear and accurate knowledge of the struggle between the Seleucids and the Jews. (See the historical outline, p. 46.)

"Apocalyptic" literature is a kind that tries to reveal the secrets of the future. Much of it is cast in bizarre symbols—the unrolling of history is described in terms of a curious statue or fights between animals.

Many apocalyptic books were written under assumed names. Ancient worthies were given credit for these writings, partly because the authors did not dare to come forth with a direct "thus saith the Lord" of their own. Hence much of the "unrolling of the future" in books like Daniel is really a review of the past—the book appears to tell of future events, but most of what it describes had really happened before the book was written. Nonetheless, the disclosure of the future remains the real interest of the writer, and he brings in the past to show how it leads up to the final end he expects. Hence the term *eschatology* (the doctrine of the end) is sometimes used as a loose synonym for apocalypse, though eschatology is a broader term. The apocalyptic writers were pessimistic about the present and expected the end to be a great overturning of things as they were, while eschatology includes a great variety of views about the end.

For instance, the prophetic writings include an eschatological note in their faith that in the future God will win a great victory. But apocalyptic literature looks at the future in a different mood from that of the prophets. Where the prophet had seen the future as a confrontation with God that would summon all the energies of the self and the community to obedience, the apocalyptic writer could "sit back" and speculate about the future. He might try to describe the future existence after the judgment (though there is not much of this in Daniel) or to forecast the date of the coming end—a type of speculation that does occur in Daniel. A further, more speculative element in apocalyptic writing is the attempt to discern some logical pattern in the succession of the great empires —what we would call "world history." The prophets had striven with the meaning of this wider history, for the most part at least, only as it impinged on the life of their community.

Like the prophets, then, the apocalyptic writers believed that a just and merciful God would determine the end of history, especially the history of the chosen people. Unlike most of the prophets, however, these writers believed that God's people were relatively righteous, and instead of condemning them they promised their deliverance. An even stronger contrast with the prophets is their view that the world is the field of a vast struggle between God and an opposing power. At present, evil is in control. God permits this—Daniel does not try to explain why (other similar books here bring in the devil). History does not *now* reflect God's justice, much less his mercy. This extreme pessimism about the present throws the writer's interest forward to the future. God must intervene, end history as we now know it, and establish a new kind of world in which His will can be done. The author of the book of Daniel seems to have expected this new world to be on earth (Chapter 7), but he does not try to describe it in detail. Other apocalyptic writers give strange pictures of the ideal world they expect. Thus the apocalyptic writings combine a real and powerful challenge to faith in the holy God with speculation that is often rather curious.

The book of Daniel presents a definite faith in real life after death. By a resurrection (renewal of life) God will enable some of the dead to participate in the life of the blessed community He will set up in the end. Thus faith in the power of God's love for His people was the basis of Jewish belief in a future life, and those who would be resurrected were pictured as living in the ideal community, after a judgment that was just and sure. Faith in the resurrection of the dead at the final end of history became the belief of most Jews during the two centuries before Christ, and Christians adopted it. The picture of a final, bodily resurrection was sturdily held even in the face of the seemingly more "spiritual" belief in the immortality of the soul that Jews and Christians found among the Greeks. Jews and early Christians insisted on resurrection rather than immortality because they understood resurrection as a gift of God, overcoming the fatal threat of death against man's existence; because they believed that in resurrection God would make possible full, active, personal life in the new existence; and because their hope was for the completion of God's people and not simply a hope for the individual. Immortality of the soul suggested to them that eternal life automatically belonged to the soul and did not have to be specially given by God; it suggested that the new existence was only a partial, almost impersonal survival; and that it was solitary rather than social. Resurrection rather than immortality thus became the form in which Jews and early Christians understood their hope of a new life after death.

There are numerous apocalyptic insertions in the prophetic books. The most extensive are Zechariah 9-14 and Isaiah 24-27. In addition, Joel could well be grouped with the apocalyptic rather than with the prophetic books. The speculative element in apocalyptic literature, which is seen in the attempt to predict the date of the end and to picture the conditions of the end, reaches far more elaborate proportions in apocalyptic books such as Enoch and the Apocalypse of Baruch, which were not included in the Old Testament or the Apocrypha.

Readings

i

Daniel 1:1-6:28.

1. What religious response do these stories glorify?
2. In what situation would this response need to be recalled?

ii

Daniel 2:26-49.

1. How many kingdoms are foreseen?
2. Is the final act, which destroys the statue, an act of God or man?
3. Is the kingdom of Nebuchadnezzar greater or less than the ones that will follow it?
4. How is the final kingdom different from those that precede it?

iii

Daniel 7:1-28.

1. Compare with the vision of Chapter 2. Does this one cover the same ground?
2. Notice "one like a man" in verse 13. Literally, this is "one like a son of man." What is the point of contrast between the four beasts and the manlike figure?
3. What does the one like a man represent?
4. For whom is the final kingdom?
5. Where will it be?

iv

Daniel 8:1-27.

1. At what point in history does the vision start?
2. At what point does it stop?
3. Why are the ram and he-goat named and the little horn left ambiguous?

v

Daniel 9:1-27.

1. What understanding of God and of the people is expressed in the prayer of Daniel?

2. The "seventy years" (verses 2, 23-27) are from Jeremiah 25:11-12; 29:10. How are they reinterpreted in Daniel 9:23-27?
3. If this calculation had been literally and exactly correct, when would the end have come?
4. Does the discrepancy in this calculation show anything about the exactness of the author's knowledge of earlier history his ability to calculate the time of the final end?

vi

Daniel 10:1-12:13.

1. Does God Himself speak to Daniel?
2. Does God directly control the actions of the nations (note Daniel 10:13, 20-21)?
3. How do you explain the detail in which the history of the Ptolemies (the kings of the south) and the Seleucids (the kings of the north) is described?

Daniel 11:21.

4. Who is the "contemptible person"?

Daniel 11:34.

5. What sort of help did the chosen people actually receive in this crisis? (See pp. 46-47.)

Daniel 12:1-4.

6. Do these events directly follow the destruction of the contemptible person?

vii

Daniel 12:1-4.

1. For whom is a future life promised?
2. What is its nature?
3. Compare with Daniel 2:44-45; 7:27. Is the new life part of the kingdom or something different?

Isaiah 25:8; 26:14-19.

4. Compare with the future life described in Daniel.

   Job 14:1-22; 19:21-27. Ecclesiastes 3:19; 9:2-6; 10. Psalms 6; 49.

5. Compare these passages with the above. Does any of them affirm a belief in a future life in communion with God?

viii

1. Compare the message of Daniel with that of the prophets.

Read one of the following:

Anderson, *Understanding the Old Testament,* pp. 508-530.

Bewer and Kraeling, *Literature of the Old Testament,* pp. 434-447.

Gottwald, *A Light to the Nations,* pp. 524-533.

10

The Background of the New Testament

alestine in New Testament times was a small but important part of the Roman empire. Roman control of the whole Mediterranean area had been achieved in the second and first centuries B.C., and Rome's intervention in Palestine was an inevitable aspect of its expanding political power. Palestine, though small and not particularly productive, was situated on important trade routes; it was near Egypt, which became an important source of food for Italy; and it was practically on the eastern frontier of the area of Roman control.

In 63 B.C. the Roman general Pompey intervened in Palestine by deposing the last Hasmonean king, Aristobulus II. This action was an attempt to end a war between Aristobulus II and his older brother Hyrcanus, whom Aristobulus had replaced. Pompey broke off the predominantly non-Jewish parts of the Hasmonean kingdom and left Judea to Hyrcanus, who was allowed to continue as high priest and local ruler, but was denied the title "king." Two decades of restlessness and civil war followed this change, since Aristobulus and his followers would not accept the Roman de-

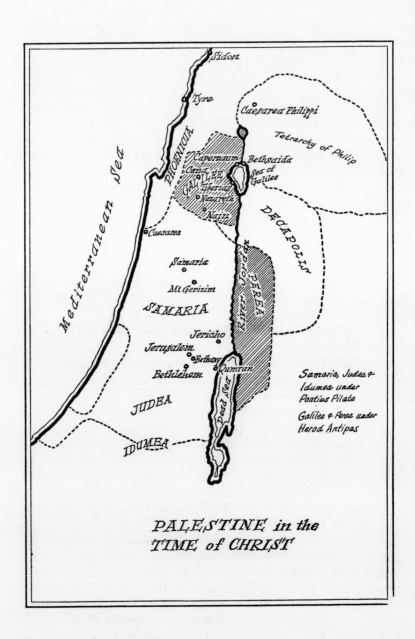

PALESTINE in the
TIME of CHRIST

cision. Supporting Hyrcanus was the Idumean (or Edomite), Antipater, who gradually emerged as the most powerful figure in Palestine.

The Romans saw that the Jewish house of the Hasmoneans would not support Roman rule, and finally, in 40 B.C., designated Herod, the son of Antipater, as king of Judea. After three years of fighting against the last of the Hasmoneans, Herod established himself as king in 37 B.C. Herod the Great, as he is called, strengthened his position by ruthless methods, including the murder of various opponents and even of three of his own sons, whom he suspected of plotting against him. He defended Roman interests and maintained friendly relations with various powerful Romans, including Octavian, who became the Roman emperor Augustus. Like Solomon, Herod was a great builder. Most of his buildings were modeled on Roman lines, but his greatest "public work" was the rebuilding of the Jewish Temple, which he made famous for its splendor. Even this project, however, could not gain the favor of his Jewish subjects. They regarded him as a foreigner and would not willingly accept the loss of their own Jewish state.

At his death in 4 B.C., Herod's kingdom was divided among his sons. Archelaus received Judea, Samaria, and Idumea; Antipas received Galilee and a strip of Transjordan; and Philip received an area north and east of the Sea of Galilee. Antipas (4 B.C.—39 A.D.), who was never popular with his subjects, and Philip (4 B.C.—34 A.D.), who was well-liked in his predominantly non-Jewish territory, were given the lesser title, "tetrarch," rather than the dignity of "king." Archelaus, who had received the central part of his father's kingdom, was the least successful of the three, and he was removed by the Romans in 6 A.D. After this his territory was governed directly by a Roman administration under an official with the title of procurator. The best known of the procurators was Pontius Pilate (26—36 A.D.).

Thus during the ministry of Jesus (a short period of only a few years, about 30 A.D.), Palestine was divided, with Judea and Samaria under a Roman procurator, Galilee under Antipas (who also controlled "Perea," a strip of Transjordan), and an area northeast of the Sea of Galilee under Philip. East and south of the Sea of Galilee was a fourth division, the Decapolis. This section was a federation of Hellenistic cities, and its existence is a reminder that Palestine was far from solidly Jewish.

The divisions in the map of Palestine reflect the Roman practice of trying to allow a good deal of local freedom to the varieties of culture within the empire. However, they could not satisfy the Jews, whose desire for independence was sparked by the tie between nation and faith. For a brief period (41—44 A.D.) Palestine was united under Herod Agrippa I, a grandson of Herod the Great. After his death his kingdom reverted to direct Roman rule, and the next twenty years saw increasing tension between the procurators and the Jewish people. In 66 A.D. a bitter revolt broke out. By 70 A.D. the Romans had subdued Palestine. Jerusalem and its Temple were destroyed. Except for a desperate revolt in 132—135 A.D., the destruction of Jerusalem marked the end of the last attempt to create a Jewish state until modern times. Recent discoveries at Muraba'at near the Dead Sea have uncovered some actual letters and documents from this final revolt.

Judaism in the time of Jesus was a "worldwide" religion. A large Jewish settlement still existed in Babylonia, but most Jews lived within the Roman empire. There were more of them outside of Palestine than in it; the largest single group lived in Alexandria. Smaller Jewish settlements were scattered throughout the Mediterranean area. On the whole these groups of the dispersion or diaspora (that is, the Jews who lived outside of Palestine) were strongly loyal to the law. But they were also subject to constant contact with the Hellenistic culture, which had spread through the whole eastern Roman empire, and to a greater or less degree they were influenced by it. Hence Judaism outside of Palestine is usually called Hellenistic Judaism. Most Hellenistic Jews spoke Greek and read the Old Testament in the Septuagint. They adopted many things from the culture that surrounded them—for instance, architecture, forms of social and religious organization, and much of Greek education and popular philosophy. The best-known thinker of Hellenistic Judaism was Philo of Alexandria, a contemporary of Paul, whose thought combined Judaism and Greek philosophy.

Hellenistic Judaism remained firm in its monotheism and in its demanding moral code. The Jews were often unpopular because of their refusal to be assimilated to prevailing cultural and religious standards. But their religion was attractive to many earnest seekers, and during the first century B.C. and the greater part of the first century A.D., many became proselytes (converts) to Judaism, and an even larger number were "inquirers" or "God-fearers" who learned from it and reverenced the Jewish God, though they did not take the final step of circumcision and full membership in the Jewish community. As Christianity spread outside Palestine, its early contacts with the pagan world were mainly through the groups of gentiles who heard Christian preaching in the synagogues.

Within Palestine itself, Judea and Galilee were predominantly Jewish, while between them were the Samaritans, a Jewish sect that did not get along well with standard Judaism. Hellenistic influence was less strong in Palestine and was consciously resisted, though it was by no means absent. Aramaic, the language of the Syrians, had become the spoken language of Palestine. It was, however, so similar to Hebrew that it was not difficult for an interested person to learn enough Hebrew to read his Scriptures.

The Temple, magnificently rebuilt by Herod the Great, served as a kind of emotional center for Judaism. Jewish people came in great numbers to visit Jerusalem, especially at the great festivals of Passover, which commemorated the deliverance from Egypt, and Pentecost, which had come to be a memorial of the giving of the law. From these visitors and from the Jewish citizens of Palestine the Temple received an enormous revenue; it was a kind of bank or treasury for Judaism. The Temple, including both its ritual and its finances, was controlled by the Sadducees. The high priests of the Temple and a small group of wealthy landowners made up the nucleus of this aristocratic group. They favored cooperation with Rome and held that the written law should be observed but kept to a minimum. They did not accept the new belief in resurrection and in general were unsympathetic with the hopes of Jewish eschatology.

Throughout Palestine (as indeed throughout the dispersion) the local center of Jewish life was the synagogue. Unlike the Temple, the synagogue was a layman's institution; any group of Jewish men could organize one. Primarily serving as a center of worship and interpretation of the Law, the synagogue often served also as social center, school, court, and inn.

In Palestine the Law continued to serve as the constitution of the Jewish community. Hence, in spite of the Sadducees' preference for keeping the Law to a minimum, it was continually necessary to reinterpret its commandments in order to take account of new circumstances. The dominant school of interpretation was that of the Pharisees, a group of earnest and humanitarian people, whose outlook on life in many ways reminds one of the Puritans. They held aloof from politics and did not favor cooperation with Rome. The "oral law," or unwritten interpretation of the Law, produced by Pharisee scholars attempted to relate the written Law to new conditions and to modify some of its harsher aspects. However, the method of the Pharisees was thoroughly legalistic. In such a matter as Sabbath observance their ideal left little to the judgment of the individual, but provided him in advance with a detailed list of *do*'s and *don't*'s. The Pharisees were believers in the resurrection of the dead, and at least some of them were interested in the whole range of eschatological hope. However, their main interest remained the Law. Their enthusiasm for a community guided by God's law provided a pattern for Jewish life that was able to survive the catastrophe of Roman destruction in 70 A.D. Medieval Judaism and modern orthodox Judaism grew from Pharisaic Judaism.

The greater part of the Jewish population of Palestine were neither Pharisees nor Sadducees. They were simply the common people—"the people of the land." As in any other group, there was great variety among the Jewish people of Palestine, but the Pharisees remained the most popular and most respected group, even among many who did not follow them in their rigor and exclusiveness.

Judaism in the time of Jesus was a religion in which there was room for tremendous variety. Besides the Pharisees and Sadducees, mentioned in the gospels as the most significant leaders of Judaism, there were many other groups with special interests of their own. The Zealots were in a sense the successors of those who had resisted the Seleucids—they stood for forceful resistance to Rome. This group captured the enthusiasm of Palestine in 66 A.D. but was unable to succeed in resisting Rome.

The Essenes, a group not mentioned in the New Testament but described by Josephus, are closely related to the Qumran community which produced the Dead Sea Scrolls. Either the two groups are identical, or the Qumran group was within the broader Essene type. The discovery of the Dead Sea Scrolls, in 1947 and the following years, has stimulated interest in these Jewish groups that tried to withdraw from sharing in the normal life of society. Many questions about the Qumran community are not yet answered, but it is clear that its dualism, or division of the world into two contending realms of good and evil, was a dualism of the Jewish apocalyptic type. Men withdrew from normal social life into such a community, turned over their property to the group, and probably renounced marriage as well to devote themselves, as the true "remnant," to a rigorous obedience to the Law, while they waited for the coming of the end and the terrible judgment that God would visit upon a wicked world.

Apocalyptic books such as Daniel and Enoch were read and preserved at Qumran, which, along with other such separated communities, may have been the principal source of apocalyptic writings. The apocalyptic faith in the imminence of a great new action of God was one of the elements in the background of Jesus that led directly into his message and helps us to see what it meant to its original hearers. It is completely unknown, however, whether or not Jesus, or for that matter John the Baptist, had had any direct contact with Qumran. For Old Testament studies the Qumran discoveries are also of great importance, for they have provided scholars with the oldest known manuscripts of the Old Testament.

Readings

Read one of the following:

The Interpreter's Bible, Vol. VII, pp. 100-113.

Kee and Young, *Understanding the New Testament,* pp. 28-45.

Price, *Interpreting the New Testament,* pp. 31-84.

Wright and Fuller, *The Book of the Acts of God,* pp. 217-252.

11

The Synoptic Gospels

Jesus was remembered because in him men saw God at work. The "good news" that God had made Himself known in Jesus, the Messiah (the Christ), was the Christian message. We know about his career and his teaching because Jesus was the subject of the early Christian preaching and teaching.

At first there were no written records of Jesus. At the center of the Christian memory of him was the death and resurrection, in which Christians saw the decisive focus of God's action in Jesus. Some forms of the Christian message concentrated so sharply on the death and resurrection that they had little need for the memories of Jesus' words and actions. Paul's letters, which are the earliest Christian writings, are of this sort. Only on a few points does Paul refer to the tradition or "account" that he "received" and "passed on." [1] But other forms of the message made great use of the words and deeds of Jesus. For these Christians, too, the death and resurrection was the focus of memory, and this part of the story is the climactic center of interest in all four gospels. But the gospels set this climactic center in a framework of Jesus' ministry to show how

[1] I Corinthians 11:23-25; 15:3-7.

118

the whole ministry, death, and resurrection are, for faith, all of one piece, all manifesting the same paradoxical power-in-weakness or victory-in-defeat.

Apparently, in the early period the words and deeds of Jesus were remembered and used in short units, so that the extended picture of the ministry was constructed later, when the gospels were written. In the early period, a short narrative climaxing in a word of Jesus, a parable, a short pithy saying, or a story of healing would be remembered and used for its own independent witness to the power that the community saw in Jesus. It seems likely that at first the function of all these brief units was in the proclamation of the faith; gradually, as there came to be a group of new converts who needed to be educated in their faith, there came to be a partial separation into two types of use: the words of Jesus were more and more used in Christian teaching, in instructing the new Christians, while the deeds of Jesus continued to be used primarily in preaching, in proclaiming the message. But the distinction was not a rigid one.

About a generation after the death of Jesus the process of writing down these memories began. No copy of the first written collection of Jesus' sayings now exists, but scholars hold that there was such a collection and that it was used as a source by the writers of both Matthew and Luke. Hence this now lost collection of Jesus' sayings is labelled Q from the German *Quelle,* meaning source.

Also, about a generation after the death of Jesus, the story of Jesus' ministry was written down, and this writing we now know as the Gospel according to Mark, the earliest of the gospels. Probably written in Rome, Mark is usually dated about 65 A.D. Although written in very simple Greek, the book is carefully planned to show how in Jesus' work God won a victory over the various sorts of opposition that he confronted.

About 80 A.D., probably in Syria or Palestine, a Jewish Christian author wrote the Gospel according to Matthew. He combined the story of Jesus' career (which he took from Mark) with Jesus' teachings (from Q), thus producing a much fuller account of Jesus and a book that has probably been the most read Christian book. He showed how Jesus had fulfilled the prophecies of the Old Testament, had given a new teaching to replace that of Moses, and yet had turned to the gentile world. Thus the author dealt with the perplexities raised in the minds of Jewish Christians by the rapid spread of Christianity among gentiles and by the destruction of Jerusalem in 70 A.D.

Probably a little later, still another author combined the story of Mark with the teachings of Q. His book, the Gospel according to Luke, is planned very differently from Matthew. For Luke the central emphasis is on God's deliverance and the coming of God's Spirit. To his volume on God at work in Jesus this author added another, the book of Acts, which traces the story of God's Spirit at work in the church. When the four gospels were gathered into one collection, Acts was separated from Luke, and it now follows the gospel collection in the New Testament.

These three gospels (Matthew, Mark, and Luke) are known as the synoptic gospels, because they give a common picture of Jesus. Each has its special literary and doctrinal interests, but all present a similar portrait of Jesus—because all were drawing on a common tradition of Jesus' acts and words, chosen for its importance to the church. Together these three books give us the best material for beginning an understanding of the work and message of Jesus.

The Ministry of Jesus

Readings

JOHN THE BAPTIST

Mark 1:1-8. Matthew 3:1-12. Luke 3:1-20.

1. What is the subject of John's preaching?
2. On what basis does he put qualification for approval by God?
3. Compare John's message with that of eighth-century prophets. How is it like their message, and at what points is it like that of the apocalyptic writings?

BAPTISM AND TEMPTATION OF JESUS

Mark 1:9-13. Matthew 3:13-4:11. Luke 3:21-4:13.

1. Note variations in the account of the baptism.
2. What interest do the gospel writers show in the relation between Jesus and John? What do they see in his baptism?

3. How do you think the gospel writers found out about the temptations?
4. Would this account for the form of the record?
5. Taking into consideration the hope for the Kingdom and the idea of the Messiah that were current in Jesus' day, state in your own words the problem involved in the temptations.

MIRACLES

i

Mark (entire book).

1. Note how Mark emphasizes Jesus' authority.
2. About what per cent of Mark's gospel would remain if you removed all accounts of miracles?
3. About what per cent of the miracles are healing?
4. Are there any duplications?

ii

Mark 1:21-39.

1. What was the first reaction of the people of Capernaum to Jesus' teachings?
2. Do you think they were talking about the "sermon" as they left the synagogue?
3. Why did Jesus leave the town the next morning?

iii

Mark 5:21-43; 7:31-37; 8:22-26; 9:14-29; 6:1-6; 8:11-13.

1. What was the prerequisite to healing?
2. Did Jesus seek to perform miracles before crowds?
3. Why was Jesus unable to heal many in Nazareth?
4. Did Jesus think of his healing as proof of his messiahship?
5. Did Mark consider the healings such proof?

iv

Mark 9:14-29; 9:38-39. Matthew 10:5-15. Luke 10:1-20. Acts 3:1-10; 8:13; 9:32-35; 13:6-12.

1. Why did Jesus rebuke the disciples who could not heal the boy?
2. Did Jesus think of his ability to heal as limited to himself?

V

1. In the light of the above, state how Jesus' "mighty works" were understood to testify to God's work in him.

The Death of Jesus

Mark 14-15.

1. Why did the priestly leaders need the help of Judas Iscariot?
2. Was Jesus surprised by the turn of events?
3. What does the Last Supper suggest about Jesus' hope for his disciples?
4. What brought about Jesus' arrest?
5. What brought about Jesus' execution? What was the charge against him?
6. Notice how the story of Jesus' death has been told with constant reference to Old Testament prophecy.

The Resurrection

I Corinthians 15:1-8. Mark 16:1-8. Luke 24:1-53. Matthew 28:1-20.

1. Which of these accounts was written first?
2. Does Paul make any distinction between the appearances to the other apostles and the appearance to him?
3. How does Paul's list of appearances compare with the appearances listed in the gospels?
4. Where does Jesus appear to the disciples in Luke?
5. Where does he appear to the disciples in Matthew?
6. For the meaning of this event to Jesus' followers, see especially the chapters on the expansion of Christianity and on Paul.

Read one of the following:

The Interpreter's Bible, Vol. VII, pp. 114-144.

Kee and Young, *Understanding the New Testament,* pp. 77-107 and 141-175.

Price, *Interpreting the New Testament,* pp. 220-235, 251-265, and 287-304.

Wright and Fuller, *The Book of the Acts of God,* pp. 261-266 and 272-280.

The Message of Jesus

Jesus' "teaching" was a proclamation of the Kingdom and the will of God. The modern habits of analysis and abstract statement were completely foreign to his mind. Nowhere did he define a term. Like the prophets and wise men of the Old Testament, Jesus proclaimed his truths concretely, with an illustration, a story, a proverb, or a question. He did not teach many things. A few great themes recur in many forms in his message. Again, in contrast to many modern teachers, Jesus did not care to impart information for its own sake. He challenged men to decision: *God rules; obey him!*

The proclamation of God's Kingdom or rule is a call to obedience, an obedience with nothing held back. Jesus refused to lay down laws that all men could follow. Each must decide what obedience means in his own case. To be a disciple means to obey God wholeheartedly; what God asks is that each man live not for himself but for his neighbor. Yet this stern demand was for Jesus the gateway to life.

The setting of Jesus' radical claim for obedience to God is the proclamation of the coming of the Kingdom of God. Like the apocalyptic writers, Jesus saw the struggle between good and evil as a struggle between God and the demonic forces of evil—a struggle that is approaching its end in a great divine victory. Unlike many of the apocalyptic writers, Jesus was not interested in speculating about or visualizing the divine victory. Rather did he focus attention on the God whose rule is coming: a God of glory and power, a God whose claim for obedience and authority of judgment are inescapable, but above all a God whose spontaneous, forgiving love extends the opportunity of fellowship to the outcast, the sinner, the failure. Jesus' message as presented in the synoptic gospels has little to say about himself. The emphasis falls on the Kingdom, which is "breaking in" or "dawning" in his ministry. Thus he saw himself and his work as called on to play a decisive role in the coming of God's Kingdom, a role that, after the resurrection, Christians identified as that of "Messiah" (see pp. 62-63). Discovering the exact form of Jesus' words about himself is one of the difficult tasks of New Testament study [see below, the last section of the *Readings* (The Son of Man)].

Because of their concrete and picturesque quality it is difficult to separate and classify the sayings of Jesus. It is virtually impossible to say "Here Jesus speaks of the Kingdom, here he speaks of the law, and here of wealth." The "good news" was a new truth, not a collection of new truths. So each saying and each parable contains, in a way, all of the gospel, although to neglect any of them is to sacrifice some insight into his message. Recognizing this, we will bow to our analytical habits by classifying his teachings, but recognize the nature of the teachings by including many passages in more than one classification.

Readings

The best-known collection of the sayings of Jesus is the "Sermon on the Mount." Some think of it as a single discourse. Others feel that it is an organized collection of sayings. The following "harmony" of the sermon, based on Matthew, indicates why there is this difference of opinion.

Mark	Matthew	Luke
	5:3-12	6:20-26
9:50	5:13-16	14:34-35
	5:17-20	16:17
	5:21-26	12:57-59
9:43-47	5:27-30	
10:11-12	5:31-32	16:18
	5:33-37	
	5:38-48	6:27-36
	6:1-4	
	6:5-8	
11:25	6:9-15	11:2-4
	6:16-18	
	6:19-21	12:33-34
	6:22-23	11:34-35
	6:24	16:13
	6:25-34	12:22-31
4:24	7:1-2	6:37-38
	7:3-5	6:41-42
	7:6	
	7:7-11	11:9-13
	7:12	6:31
	7:13-14	13:24
	7:15-16	
	7:17-20	6:43-45
	7:21-23	6:46
	7:24-27	6:47-49

1. How much of the sermon is found in Mark?
2. How much is omitted in Luke?
3. Do you think Matthew's or Luke's presentation of the material is the more easy to learn?
4. Were Matthew's and Luke's sources exactly alike?
5. Do the differences in Matthew and Luke ever result in different meanings?
6. Which author is more concerned with the poor and sick?
7. Which is more concerned with the law?
8. Is this message based on a "higher common sense" or on an understanding of the uncompromising will of God?

Indicate the division points that would distribute the sermon, as recorded in Matthew, according to the following outline:

A. Discipleship
    a. Qualifications
    b. Value to the world
B. Place of the law
    a. Eternal value
    b. Inadequacies of specific laws
C. Place of ritual worship
    a. Alms
    b. Prayer
    c. Fasting
D. Value of discipleship
E. Various admonitions and warnings
F. Inevitability of reward and punishment

1. Do you think this sort of outline comes from Jesus, from the author of Matthew, or from chance?
2. Can you improve the outline?
3. At what points is it most difficult to outline the material?

The following classification of the teachings of Jesus is based on the above outline. Whatever value it has depends on its success in gathering together groups of sayings whose major emphasis is on one subject.

THE KINGDOM

i

*Mark 1:14-15. Matthew 5:3, 10, 19, 20; 6:10; 7:21;
13:11, 19, 24, 31, 33.*

1. What do Mark and Matthew say was the subject of Jesus' message?

2. Do these references deal with a "Kingdom" in the sense of a place or a group of people? What aspect of the Kingdom do they stress?

ii

Matthew 5:1-12, 33-48; 18:1-6, 21-35.
Luke 10:25-37.

1. Did Jesus base discipleship on racial or legal qualifications?
2. Does one qualify for discipleship on the basis of what one does or what one is?
3. Do the Beatitudes (Matthew 5:1-12) list different kinds of people who will be disciples or the different qualities of disciples?
4. Describe a disciple.

iii

(a) *Mark 10:6; 12:17; 14:32-42.*
Matthew 5:45.

1. Did Jesus attempt to prove the existence of God or to define God? Would the background of his audience explain this?
2. What did Jesus see as the proper response of the creature, man, to the Creator, God?
3. What does the metaphor "Kingdom of God" imply about God?

(b) *Mark 1:15. Matthew 7:2; 25:1-13,*
14-30, 31-46.

1. In what way do these passages speak of God?
2. What bases of judgment are presented?
3. Why do both the "sheep" and the "goats" show surprise in Jesus' picture of the judgment? Compare with Matthew 7:21-23.
4. Do the traditional religious practices (law, ritual) come into the picture of the judgment? If so, how?

(c) *Matthew 6:9; 7:7-11; 18:14.*
Luke 15:11-32.

1. In what way do these passages speak of God? How do you relate these statements to those in Sections (a) and (b) above?
2. Does God's goodness depend on the goodness of the ones He loves?
3. Does God's goodness place more or less exacting demands upon man than would a God of sheer justice?

iv

(a) *Matthew 11:2-19; 13:16-17. Luke 11:17-20; 16:16.*
(b) *Mark 4:26-29. Matthew 13:31-33.*
(c) *Luke 12:35-40; 17:20-21. Mark 9:1; 13:32.*
Matthew 13:24-43, 47-50; 25:31-46.

1. Did Jesus expect the Kingdom to come suddenly or to develop slowly?
2. Is the Kingdom present in Jesus' proclamation?
3. Is it to come in the future?
4. How do you relate the present to the future in his message about the Kingdom?

v

Matthew 8:5-13; 10:5-7, 23; 15:21-28; 21:42-22:14.

1. Did Jesus think of the Kingdom as limited to Jews?

THE LAW

i

Matthew 5:17-19; 23:1-12. Luke 16:19-31.

1. Did Jesus repudiate the law?
2. Did he advise disobedience?
3. How did he evaluate the law and the prophets in the story of the rich man and Lazarus?

ii

Matthew 5:21-48—Deuteronomy 5:6-21. Matthew 5:31-32; Mark 10:2-9—Deuteronomy 24:1, 3. Matthew 5:43-48; Mark 12:28-34—Deuteronomy 6:5; Leviticus 19:17-18. Matthew 5:33-37; 23:16-22—Numbers 30:2.

1. Can you relate Jesus' teachings here to Matthew 5:17-19?
2. Would one who followed Jesus' teachings break the laws recorded in the Torah?
3. Note Mark 10:4-5. What would be the expected reaction of Jesus' hearers to this freedom of interpretation of the law?
4. Is "hate your enemy" an accurate quotation of the law?
5. Does the law provide for a system of oaths as indicated in Matthew 23:16-22?

iii

Mark 1:40-44—Leviticus 14. Mark 7:1-23; Matthew 15:1-20—Leviticus 11. Mark 2:23-28; Matthew 12:1-14—Deuteronomy 5:12-15.

1. Did Jesus distinguish between the ritual and moral laws?
2. Did he "declare all food clean" as Mark says in 7:19?
3. Did he distinguish between written law and traditions in regard to foods? in regard to leprosy?
4. State the meaning of Mark 2:27.
5. Did Jesus relate his freedom of action to the coming of the Kingdom?

THE RITUAL

i

Matthew 6:1-4; 6:5-15; 6:16-18.

1. Did the general principle found in Mark 2:27 apply to alms, prayer, and fasting in the mind of Jesus?

ii

a

Mark 1:35; 6:46; 9:29. Luke 3:21; 5:16; 23:46; 10:21-22; 9:18, 28-29; 22:41-42.

1. Was prayer a constant practice with Jesus?
2. Did he use memorized prayers? Did he pray "in the synagogues and on the street corners"?
3. Did his prayers come at times of stress and need?

b

Matthew 7:7-11. Luke 11:1-13. Mark 11:22-25; 12:38-40. Luke 18:9-14. Matthew 6:14-15.

1. What is God's attitude toward those who pray?
2. What attitude toward God makes prayer effective?
3. What attitude toward man is required of him who prays?
4. Is prayer active or passive?
5. Is the one who prays to do anything else?

c

Matthew 5:44; 9:35-38. Luke 6:28; 22:31-32.

1. Did Jesus believe in intercessory prayer?
2. Is there a difference between the synoptics and John (see John 17:1-26) on this question?

iii

Matthew 6:16-18. Mark 2:18-22. Luke 4:1-2.

1. Did Jesus teach his disciples not to fast?
2. Did Jesus ever fast?
3. State the meaning of the parables of the new patch and the new wine skins.
4. Can you substitute "fasting" for "sabbath" in Mark 2:27 without doing violence to Jesus' teaching?

iv

Matthew 23:1-39. Luke 14:1-6. Matthew 5:23-24.

1. In the light of these and your other readings under "the law" and "the ritual":
   (a) What is the criticism that Jesus makes of law and cultic practices?
   (b) To what was the ritual subordinate in Jesus' thinking?
   (c) What values did Jesus see in the ritual?

THE VALUE OF THE KINGDOM

i

Matthew 6:19-34; 13:44-46; 18:8-9. Luke 9:57-62; 14:26-35; 16:19-31; 18:18-30; 19:1-10; 21:1-4.

1. In Matthew 6:21, what is meant by "heart"?
2. What did Jesus mean by "treasures in heaven"?
3. What is the meaning of the parables of the treasure and the pearl?
4. How does it fit into Jesus' warning to those who would follow him?
5. Did Jesus demand vows of poverty?
6. Why did he demand "all" from the rich young ruler and accept "half" from Zaccheus?

VARIOUS ADMONITIONS AND WARNINGS

i

Matthew 7:1-12; 12:22-37.

1. What did the Pharisees do or say that involved the Holy Spirit?
2. Was Jesus angry because of what they said about him?
3. On what basis were they judging? How does such judging involve being judged?

ii

Luke 10:25-37; 15:11-32.

1. Do these stories seem to be simple parables or allegories?
2. If they are interpreted as parables, what is the point of each?
3. Is the "Prodigal Son" or the "Forgiving Father" the better title for Luke 15:11-32? Why?

REWARD AND PUNISHMENT

Matthew 5:45; 7:13-14; 7:24-27; 20:1-16. Luke 17:5-10.

1. Did Jesus think of the reward for righteousness as being on a *quid pro quo* basis?
2. Did he think of it as earned or as given?
3. Did he think of it as superimposed and separate or as an essential part of righteous living?
4. Does the parable of the houses appeal to the emotions or to common sense?
5. Toward what does the "narrow way" lead?
6. State Jesus' concept of the reward in your own words.

THE SON OF MAN

(a) *Mark 8:38; 13:26. Matthew 10:23, 32-33. Luke 12:8-9.*
(b) *Mark 2:10-11, 27-28. Matthew 8:18-20; 11:18-19. Luke 11:29-30.*
(c) *Mark 8:31; 9:9, 31; 10:33-34, 45.*

1. Who is the speaker in all of the above passages?
2. Is the Son of Man of section (a) the same as the Son of Man of section (b)? Is the answer to this question absolutely clear? How would it have been answered by the author of Matthew? Compare Matthew 10:32-33 with Luke 12:8-9.
3. Note that these Son of Man passages do not speak of the Kingdom of God.

4. Which group of passages is most likely to have been influenced by the Christian memory during the oral period?
5. What do you find to be the meaning of the term "Son of Man"?

QUESTIONS FOR DISCUSSION

1. Describe the Kingdom of God as Jesus thought of it.
2. Show how Jesus' concept of the Kingdom related to his concept of God.
3. Did Jesus expect the Kingdom to come soon?
4. Was Jesus primarily concerned with social reform? Could his teachings be applied so as to reform society?
5. By what method can his message be brought to bear upon society?
6. Show how Jesus' concept of the value of the Kingdom is related to his teachings in regard to wealth.
7. State Jesus' concept of the value and limitations of the law and ritual in your own words.
8. Was Jesus primarily concerned with belief as such? What would one *have* to believe to take his teachings seriously?
9. Did Jesus condemn the "pleasures of this world"? Did he think of selfish experiences as pleasurable? Did he really feel that discipleship meant a joyful life? If so, why "take up your cross"?
10. How do you relate Jesus' message about the coming of the Kingdom to his demand for obedience?

Read one of the following:

The Interpreter's Bible, Vol. VII, pp. 145-175.

Kee and Young, *Understanding the New Testament,* pp. 108-140.

Price, *Interpreting the New Testament,* pp. 235-250 and 265-287.

Wright and Fuller, *The Book of the Acts of God,* pp. 266-272 and 281-285.

For more detailed study, see Bornkamm, *Jesus of Nazareth.*

12

The Expansion of Christianity

hristianity is based on the faith that God raised Jesus from the dead. The early Christians remembered a group of appearances of the risen Lord to his disciples. They were convinced, too, that the Jesus they had known continued to be known in the presence of the Spirit. The group of disciples in Jerusalem grew rapidly. Of course all of them were Jews of Palestine at first, and they continued to observe the practices of their Jewish faith. In addition, they had a distinctive ceremony of their own, a meal eaten together in remembrance of Jesus and in hope of his coming again. A second ceremony, baptism, soon became a part of the group's practice.

Presently Hellenistic Jews living in Jerusalem began to be interested in the new group that claimed to have seen the beginning of the fulfillment of God's promises. The most brilliant early leader of the Hellenistic group was Stephen, who was put to death for his uncompromising attack on the Jewish leaders. A persecution of the followers of Jesus ensued, but by scattering them it served to speed the expansion of the new group. Soon groups of followers of "the Way" were formed outside of Palestine. The most important of these new

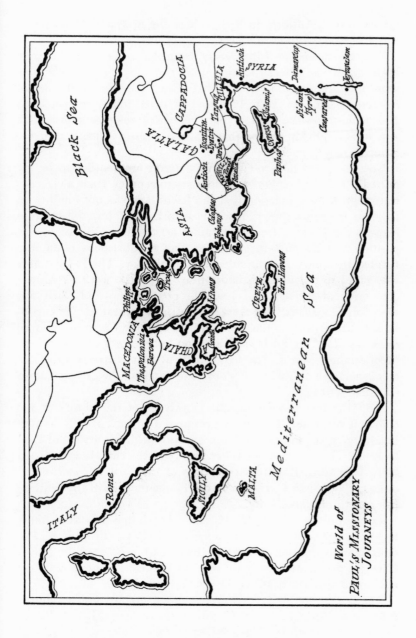

World of
Paul's Missionary
Journeys

groups was at Antioch, in Syria, where the nickname "Christians" was first given to Jesus' followers.

The expansion of Christianity from Palestine into the communities of the Greek-speaking Jews was only the prelude to a more important step. Gentiles (that is, non-Jews) began to take an interest in the new faith. The story of Peter and Cornelius (Acts 10-11) illustrates the tension that this new development produced. But it was quickly agreed that all who wished to come into the group were welcome.

Now the question arose: On what terms are gentiles to be admitted? Paul, the best-known missionary to gentiles, made a vigorous statement of his conviction that the Jewish law was not binding on the new converts; they did not have to become Jews in order to become Christians. After some rather acrimonious discussion, this position was adopted in substance, though Christians often substituted their own lists of rules for the old law. The result was a very rapid spread of Christianity into the gentile world. Within a generation of the death of Jesus the great majority of Christians were former pagans. The work of Paul was central in this expansion, but many others took part in it, taking the Christian message to Rome, to Alexandria, and to most other parts of the eastern Mediterranean world. The letters of Paul were written during this first generation of Christianity's existence and are the earliest known Christian writings.

After the first generation, our knowledge of the history of the church is very scanty for almost a century. The book of Acts, written late in the first century A.D., stops abruptly with the arrival of Paul in Rome, about 60 A.D. No other history of the church was written for a long time. But from the books of the New Testament and other early Christian writings we can fix the outlines of the continuing growth of Christianity.

Expansion continued. By 150 A.D. the church was very much larger. It had also become an almost entirely gentile church. The destruction of Jerusalem in 70 A.D. had greatly weakened the Jewish Christian group, and though it continued to exist, it never was very influential after the death of the original apostles.

The destruction of Jerusalem also raised the question of church leadership. No longer could Christians turn to the original church. Organization in the first generation was very informal; Paul, who had never seen Jesus, could become an apostle and negotiate as an equal with Peter. With the passing of time and the development of variant forms of faith, it became important to establish a standard leadership and a standard doctrine. From a very early time there was a wide variety of both faith and practice in the church. Paul allowed for great variety, though already in that early period he had to struggle against types of faith that he could not recognize as Christian. By the second century the problem was intense, especially the conflict with gnosticism. This term covers a variety of dualistic groups that made so sharp a gap between God and the world that they could not regard the world as God's creation, nor could most of them regard the life, death, and resurrection of Christ as a salvation event; Jesus was transformed into a revealer of heavenly truth. The struggle and interaction with this type of faith occupied much of the energy of the church from an early period, especially in the second century. By 150 A.D. the standard leadership of the bishops was well on its way to establishment, and belief was being standardized by creed and canon. From the middle of the second century, the life and thought of the church had lost much of the flexibility of the early period, and those who did not conform to the established standards were excluded from the organization. But standardization prevented the indiscriminate mixing of pagan and Christian ideas and made it possible for the church to grow without losing its distinctive character.

Persecution by Rome struck Christianity only sporadically during the first and early second centuries. Nero made the Christians scapegoats for a fire in Rome in 63 A.D.; tradition holds that both Peter and Paul died in this persecution. Other scattered persecutions affected Christians both in Rome and elsewhere. Though Christianity was regarded as an illegal religion, there was no general persecution until the third century.

All the New Testament books except the letters of Paul (written late in the first generation) were written during the century following the death of Paul. The synoptic gospels were composed during the generation following Paul (see above, pp. 118-120). The Gospel according to John was written close to the end of the first century. Most of the other New Testament books were written late in the first century or early in the second. Many of them reflect the problems of organization and consolidation of the church; others (such as I Peter and Revelation) reflect the persecutions arising from the growing tension between the Christians and Rome. For the history of the church, see not only the readings below, but also the chapter on Paul (Chapter 13).

Reading

i

Acts 2:1-42.

1. Study Peter's sermon. What view of Christ does it express?

Acts 2:43-47.

2. Notice the picture of the community life of the first Christians.

Acts 6:1-7.

3. Notice the beginning of different types of leadership.

Acts 10:34-43.

4. Compare the outline of Peter's sermon with the outline of the Gospel of Mark.

ii

Acts 7:54-8:3; 9:1-30; 22:3-21; 26:2-23.

1. How did Paul first come into contact with Christianity?
2. What was his reaction to it?
3. Tell the story of Paul's conversion and return to Jerusalem according to Acts.
4. Contrast the story in Galatians 1:13-2:14.
5. Why did Paul think of himself as an apostle?

iii

Acts 13:1-52.

1. Compare this account of the beginning of Paul's missionary work with the account in Galatians 1:11-2:14. Does Luke think of Paul as limiting his message to gentiles?

iv

Acts 15:1-16:15.

1. What issue arose between Paul and the church in Jerusalem?
2. Note the change from third to first person (16:10). The "we"

sections of Acts are often thought to come from a diary of Luke. (See Colossians 4:14 for a reference to Luke as a companion of Paul.)

v

Acts 18:1-24:27; 28:16-31.

1. Why is the arrival of Paul in Rome a fitting climax for the book of Acts? Was the author ignorant of what happened to Paul after this?

Read one of the following:

The Interpreter's Bible, Vol. VII, pp. 176-227.

Kee and Young, *Understanding the New Testament,* pp. 46-76, 176-231, 236-254, 262-267, and 292-309.

Price, *Interpreting the New Testament,* pp. 85-146 and 329-358.

Wright and Filson, *Westminster Atlas,* rev., pp. 95-98.

Wright and Fuller, *The Book of the Acts of God,* pp. 287-314.

13

Paul

In Paul's letters we find the most influential interpretation of the meaning of Christ. Paul relates the coming of Christ to God's work in the past, to the present experience of the Christian group, and to the hope of the future in a pattern developed from the prophetic thought of the Old Testament. God's purpose is to create a community in which men can be themselves and can really live together, but men have rebelled against His purpose and are bringing destruction on themselves. God, however, will not be frustrated in His purpose; He is carrying it through and in fact has taken the decisive step in the coming of Christ. Christ broke the barrier of man's disobedience both by making God's spontaneous, overflowing generosity decisively known to man and by offering, as a representative man, a completely obedient life to God. His resurrection inaugurated a new era in the life of men, in which God's power, at work in the fellowship of believers, makes really possible the life of self-forgetting love for which men are intended. The new life that Christians find now, through faith, is a foretaste of the eternal life that God has prepared for them. But this new life is open only to faith; to the outward eye the world is not changed, and the new life is not a possession which the believer can hold fast. It must be repeatedly renewed by the renewed decision of faith. The good news about God's great act must be proclaimed to the whole world, for God's goodness is no longer confined to the narrow bounds of an ethnic group, but in Christ is extended to all mankind. Paul himself is an "apostle," or authorized representative, of Christ and of Christ's good news.

The new thing in the pattern of Paul's thought is that God's decisive act, by which men are delivered from themselves, is not a hope but an accomplished fact. In Christ God has come to grips with the opposition that human nature sets up against His will and has overcome it. But the coming of Christ means far more to Paul than the changing of a pattern of thought. The concrete content of his faith is determined by the character of Christ. Christ's character supplies on the one hand the clue to the real nature of God—God is known to be good, even to evil men, because that generous goodness is met in Christ. On the other hand, the character of Christ supplies the key to right action. Men can and must be like him; Christ gives both a guide to and the power of goodness. Paul urges men to turn away from reliance on their own moral effort and to put their faith in the goodness of God made manifest in Christ. He is convinced that this way produces a profound transformation of character. But the transformation is not automatic; nor does the power of Christ publicly destroy the evil forces within and without with which men struggle. The Christian life is a summons to effort —strenuous, disciplined, and thoughtful obedience to God in the midst of the struggle of life. Paul believes that the effort can succeed, for the Spirit of Christ gives men a power that they can find in no other way.

Reading

Wright and Fuller, *The Book of the Acts of God*, pp. 321-356.

Romans

Romans was written when Paul was in Corinth, about 57 A.D. He had never been to Rome, where an important church had grown. Paul had spent about a decade in the lands around the Aegean Sea, and felt that he had spent long enough there. He wanted to press on to a new field, the western Mediterranean area, and he knew that the support of Rome, the key to the West, was practically necessary if he was to succeed in his new venture. He wrote Romans to introduce himself and his gospel to the church at Rome in order to enlist its backing for the new project he hoped to begin.

In Romans Paul produced the most systematic of his letters, but he was not setting forth a complete "system of doctrine." A special emphasis is given in Romans to the relationship of faith in Christ to the law, no doubt because in Rome, as in some other churches, the relationship between Christianity and Judaism was a live question.

The plan of Romans is to sketch the change that Christ makes in men's lives. Paul held that, apart from Christ, man's life and work have no real outcome or permanent result. Man's striving is made futile by his prideful refusal to acknowledge the lordship of God. Attempting to direct his own life, man finds himself in the grip of sin, which is both the result of his own choice and an inescapable power that holds him. Even where the Law, that is, the Old Testament Law, enters the human picture, it does not bring man out of his hopeless situation. The Law points out to men the things that God really wants them to do, and the sum of its requirements is love. But the Law only makes man's problem more difficult, first by intensifying his awareness of sin in the light of its clear standard and then by stimulating his egotistic pride to attempt to make himself good enough to deal with God. Thus men who live by the Law are not really able to live in obedience to God.

For Paul, faith in Christ furnished the way out of this dilemma. In Christ God condescends to come down to man's level and come to grips with his problem. Christ's victory over sin and death are God's victory, and they can become available to every man. By faith man is enabled to come into God's presence. By virtue of his identification with Christ God counts him just, and a new inner power, the presence of Christ or the Spirit, enables him at last to live and to accomplish that for which God intended him.

Here the development of Paul's thought in Romans is set aside for three chapters (Chapters 9-11) in which the relation of Israel to God's purpose is discussed. The problem is: Why have so few Jews turned to Christ? Paul states that God did choose Israel, and that since it was God's choice, not man's, man is not to complain if the outcome of God's work is not just what men expect it to be; he then reminds his readers that in the past only a remnant were faithful to the Lord and that exactly the same thing is true in his own time. His final comment on this perplexing question is rather different from these two; he points out that the disloyalty of the Jews has hastened the spread of the gospel to the rest of the world and states his faith that this insensitivity of God's people to Christ is a temporary thing, which will be overcome in due season, so that in the end "all Israel will be saved."

The concluding chapters of Romans are a practical application of what has gone before. If God, in Christ, has done so much for men, let them respond by doing the things God wants. Paul sketches the kind of action God approves and gives several concrete illustrations. These concluding chapters show how profoundly in harmony the message of the early church was with the message of Jesus.

Readings

i

Romans 1:1-17; 15:14-33.

1. What was the nature of Paul's work?
2. Did he address the Romans as if he had authority over them?
3. What was Paul's attitude toward working in churches founded by others?
4. Why could he not come to Rome directly?

ii

Romans 1:18-3:20.

1. What is the theme of this section?
2. What is the outcome of the activity of man as an individual and in society?
3. Is judgment future, present, or both?
4. How will men be tested?
5. Are all responsible? Why?
6. What has been the net result of the Law?

iii

Romans 3:21-4:25.

1. What is the theme of this section?
2. How is the vicious circle in which men find themselves broken?

3. How does the deliverance become available to men?
4. Why was it so difficult for God to make his character known?
5. In what sense did Paul "confirm the Law"?
6. How did Paul use the illustration of Abraham?
7. Could he easily have found other such illustrations in the Pentateuch?
8. Why was Paul so anxious to show that the "promise" did not depend on "the Law"?

iv

Romans 5:1-11.

1. What is the theme of this section? Compare with Romans 3:21-26.
2. What is the central difference that Christ makes?
3. Does faith put an end to the struggle of life?
4. Is there any difference between God's and Christ's attitudes toward men?
5. Is God's attitude dependent on man's attitude toward him?
6. Compare the picture of God's character and purpose presented here with that of the synoptic gospels.

Romans 5:12-21.

7. Does this message presuppose individualism or corporate life as the essence of human existence?
8. In what way is Christ like Adam?

v

Romans 6:1-7:6.

1. What weakness did some see in Paul's presentation of the gospel?
2. How did Paul answer the objection?
3. What is the source of the Christian's moral power?
4. Does the Christian have to exert his will?
5. Note the three illustrations—baptism, slavery, and marriage. Was Paul making the same point with each of them, or not?

vi

Romans 7:7-25.

1. What was the psychological effect of the Law?
2. Why did it have this effect?
3. Do you think that this section comes out of Paul's own experience? Do you think that it represents the experience of a non-

Christian, or that Paul means that all men, Christians as well as others, face inner division and struggle?
4. Are men free to act in any way they wish?
5. What provides a resolution for the impasse?

vii

Romans 8:1-39.

1. What is the theme of this section?

Romans 8:1-4.

2. Is the Spirit a part of human nature?
3. How does it come to guide a man's personality?

Romans 8:15-11.

4. What does it mean to be "physically minded"?
5. Is there any difference between "God's Spirit," "Christ's Spirit," and "Christ in your hearts"?
6. Does the raising of Christ from the dead bring men a promise of future life, a promise of life now, or both?

Romans 8:12-13.

7. Does the gift of the Spirit put an end to moral effort? Compare with Chapter 6.

Romans 8:14-17.

8. Who are "sons of God"? What does it mean to be one?

Romans 8:18-25.

9. Does faith bring escape from suffering?
10. How is suffering faced?

Romans 8:26-30.

11. What is the ground of the Christian's hope?

Romans 8:31-39.

12. How does a man find this kind of conviction?

viii

Romans 9:1-11:36.

1. What is the theme of this section? Could these chapters be omitted without breaking the continuity of thought?

Romans 9:1-5.

2. What are the privileges of the Jews?

Romans 9:6-29.

3. Can man predict how God's decisions will be made?
4. Does anyone have a right to demand favorable treatment from God?
5. Has God worked in the past through a majority of His people?
6. Did Paul think of God as the cause of evil? Was his position consistent on this point?

Romans 9:30-10:21.

7. What error prevented Judaism from inheriting the promises?
8. Could they have done otherwise?

Romans 11:1-36.

9. What precedent did Paul find for the fact that only a few Jews had faith in Christ? (Compare with 9:6-13.) What prophet formulated this teaching?
10. How does the Jewish rejection of Christ serve God's purpose?
11. Will the Jews be permanently rejected by God?
12. Compare the metaphor of the olive tree with Jesus' parables. Which displays the better understanding of nature?
13. What point was Paul making with the metaphor of the olive tree?
14. Did Paul expect that all human and spiritual powers would finally accept the Lordship of Christ?

ix

Romans 12:1-21.

1. Compare the pattern of human behavior that Paul pictured here with that of the teaching of the synoptic gospels.
2. What, for Paul, was the most important kind of worship? Compare with the prophets and with Jesus.
3. What practical points was Paul making with the metaphor of the body?
4. What kind of action characterizes all the specific examples? Compare with I Corinthians 13.
5. Compare the attitude of man pictured here with the attitude of God pictured in 5:1-11.
6. Does Paul's ethic cancel out common-sense morality? What is its relation to it?

x

Romans 13:1-14.

1. What is the function of government?
2. Do Paul's remarks apply to all governments?
3. What is the relation between the law and the Christian's ethic?
4. To what motivation did Paul appeal?

xi

Romans 14:1-15:6.

1. This is an example of how to apply the general principles of Chapters 12 and 13 to a concrete problem. Two problems are mentioned: religious vegetarianism and, rather incidentally, the observance of the Sabbath. On the food question, see also I Corinthians 8.
2. Is it important to have carefully thought out convictions about what you do?
3. Is it necessary that all arrive at the same convictions?
4. What approach did Paul suggest when there is a sincere difference of convictions?
5. Did Paul expect all Christians to agree?
6. Can a Christian make his choices as an isolated individual?
7. What is the relation of the Christian's choices to the example of Christ?

xii

Romans 15:7-13.

1. What final point did Paul make in this section, with which he ended the sketch of his gospel?
2. Did he expect social and racial distinctions to be maintained within the church?

xiii

Romans 16:1-27 (for 15:14-33, see Section i).

1. What does this chapter contain besides greetings?
2. Since some of the persons mentioned in this chapter are known to have been at one time in Asia Minor, it is often suggested that Chapter 16, though a letter of Paul, was not part of the original letter to Rome.

Read one of the following:

The Interpreter's Bible, Vol. IX pp. 355-372.

Kee and Young, *Understanding the New Testament,* pp. 268-291.

Price, *Interpreting the New Testament,* pp. 398-414.

Other Letters of Paul

Except for Romans, Colossians, and Philemon, Paul's letters were written in response to specific questions or problems that had arisen in the various churches he had founded. As a group the letters fall within the later part of Paul's ministry, approximately 50-60 A.D.

No readings beyond the New Testament itself are listed here; the student is referred to the appropriate sections of Kee and Young, *Understanding the New Testament,* or Price, *Interpreting the New Testament,* as well as the more extensive introductions to the various books in *The Interpreter's Bible,* Vols. IX-X.

Galatians

Galatians deals briefly, but in a very intense and impassioned way, with much the same range of topics Paul considered in Romans. Its date is uncertain, as is also the exact location of the churches in Galatia. Many students think this letter may be the earliest of Paul's letters and therefore the earliest Christian writing now extant. Others would date the letter somewhat later.

Galatians presents a vigorous and uncompromising statement of the independence of Christian faith from the law. Paul's conviction on this point was his most controversial belief, and evidently he had been followed in Galatia by Christian preachers who said that Paul went too far in cutting off the new faith from the old. He wrote Galatians to defend his position and to reject that of his opponents.

Readings

Galatians 1:1-6:18.

1. What issue caused Paul to write this letter?
2. What group disagreed with Paul?

3. What did Paul mean by "what they once were" in 2:6?
4. On what basis did Paul claim his authority?
5. What function had the law served?
6. Why is a "relapse" into reliance on the law so dangerous according to Paul?
7. What danger did Paul see in his position?
8. How did he guard against it?

Galatians 6:11.

9. Who wrote this? What does it imply as to the way in which the rest of the letter was written down?

I and II Thessalonians

I and II Thessalonians were written about 50 A.D. from Greece to the church at Thessalonica in Macedonia, which Paul had founded shortly before. His preaching about the coming of the end had led some of the Thessalonian Christians to become greatly concerned about the end, and eventually to become so unsettled that they could not apply themselves to their daily tasks. Paul explained different aspects of his hope in I and II Thessalonians and worked out the ethical implications of this hope.

Readings

i

I Thessalonians 1:1-5:28.

1. What was the occasion for writing this letter?
2. Where was Paul?
3. What problems were bothering the Thessalonians?
4. How did Paul deal with them?

ii

II Thessalonians 1:1-3:18.

1. Compare with I Thessalonians.

II Thessalonians 2:1-12.

2. Does this harmonize with the picture given in I Thessalonians?
3. Can you account for the difference?

4. Why has the problem of idleness arisen?
5. Had Paul anticipated it? (See I Thessalonians 2:5, 9; 5:14.)

I Corinthians

I Corinthians, written from Ephesus to Corinth about 55 A.D., is the best work in which to study Paul's understanding of the daily life of the Christian and of the church. The Corinthians had written to him to ask about some things that had been disturbing them, and he had also heard some things about the church that he did not like. The long letter covers a wide range of topics, all bound together by the conviction that faith in Christ has its prime expression in love.

Readings

I Corinthians 1:1-4:21.

1. For what virtues did Paul praise the Corinthians? Note that he did not praise their love.
2. What problem existed in the church at Corinth?
3. What was the source of Paul's teaching?
4. What was Paul's approach to the problem of factions?

I Corinthians 5:1-13.

5. What feature of Paul's teaching might be made to encourage this sort of behavior? (See Romans 6:1.)

I Corinthians 6:1-20.

6. How did Paul suggest that they settle their disputes?
7. What is the source of the idea that "I may do anything I please"? (See question 5.) How did Paul deal with this idea?

I Corinthians 7:1-40.

8. Why did Paul discuss this particular problem? (See also I Corinthians 8:1; 12:1.)
9. State his view of marriage.
10. State his view of the relation between eschatological action and concrete decision.

I Corinthians 8:1-13; 10:1-11:1.

11. State the principle. Did Paul tell them specifically what to do?

I Corinthians 9:1-27.

12. Why did Paul have to defend himself?

I Corinthians 11:2-16.

13. Was Paul here discussing custom or a matter of permanent principle?

I Corinthians 11:17-34.

14. This is Paul's only discussion of the Lord's Supper besides I Corinthians 10:14-22. Study his view of it in these two passages and note what he disapproves.
15. How did Paul understand the Lord's Supper—as a re-enactment, as the celebration of a perennial presence, or both?

I Corinthians 12:1-31; 14:1-40.

16. What was "prophecy"?
17. Why was it felt to be important?
18. Study Paul's treatment of the problem. What did he value more highly than prophecy? Why? Compare with I Corinthians 13.

I Corinthians 13:1-13.

19. Compare with Jesus' teaching on love. Is this similar in form? in content?

I Corinthians 15:1-58.

20. Note the connection between the resurrection of Christ and the general resurrection.
21. Is the resurrection just individual blessedness? What more is it?
22. Note the concluding verse of the chapter. What practical application of his faith did Paul make?

I Corinthians 16:1-24.

23. Where was Paul? What was his plan?

II Corinthians

II Corinthians, written about 57 A.D. from Macedonia, followed a vigorous disagreement between Paul and the church at Corinth. After the writing of I Corinthians a group at Corinth had rebelled against Paul's leadership, and after a brief visit he had been compelled to withdraw without re-establishing himself as the leader of the church. Then after he wrote a stern letter (see II Corinthians 2:4; 7:8, 12) the Corinthians had been reconciled to Paul's leadership. Paul wrote II Corinthians (at least Chapters 1-9) to seal their newly re-established friendship. It is probable that Chapters 10-13 are part of the stern letter written earlier.

Readings

II Corinthians 6:14-7:1.

1. Notice how this passage breaks the context. Observe the topic discussed. Could this be a part of the letter mentioned in I Corinthians 5:9-13?

II Corinthians 1:1-6:13.

2. What has happened between Paul and the Corinthians?
3. Study what Paul said about the meaning of Christ in his own experience.

II Corinthians 7:2-9:15.

4. Does the problem under discussion appear to have been solved?
5. Was the letter mentioned in II Corinthians 2:4; 7:8, 12 the one we know as I Corinthians?

II Corinthians 10:1-13:14.

6. Notice the tone of these chapters. Is it the same as in Chapters 1-9?
7. Does the problem under discussion appear to have been solved?
8. Could these chapters be the letter mentioned in II Corinthians 7:8?

II Corinthians 11:16-12:9.

9. Study this account of Paul's career. What was the driving force of his life?

Philippians

Philippians was written from prison to the church at Philippi in Macedonia, a church with which Paul had enjoyed the closest of friendly relations. He wrote to thank them for their generosity. In the course of the letter he gave a vivid picture of how he was sustained by his faith and of how Christians ought to get along with one another. If written from Rome, Philippians is a late letter, written about 60 A.D. Some think that it was written from prison in Ephesus about five years earlier. Some even hold that Philippians is made up of two or three letters of Paul.

Readings

Philippians 1:1-4:23.

1. What had happened to Paul?
2. What specific purpose did the letter serve? (See 4:10-20)
3. Compare the problems discussed with those in the letters to the Galatians and Corinthians.

Philippians 2:1-11.

4. Study this famous statement about Christ. What practical application did Paul make?

Philippians 4:8-9.

5. This is a list of virtues admired by pagans. What attitude did Paul take to the best of the pagan world?

Colossians

Colossians was written from prison, either from Rome or from Ephesus, to the church at Colossae in Asia Minor. Paul had never visited the church at Colossae, but he was evidently concerned about their faith. The wrong kind of faith that Paul opposed seems to have been a gnosticism like that opposed in the letters of John. Gnosticism denied the uniqueness of the revelation of God in Christ and did not emphasize the moral consequences of faith.

Readings

Colossians 1:1-4:18.

1. Where was Paul? Who was with him? (See 4:7-18.)
2. Study the wrong ideas and practices he was seeking to correct.

3. Study the statements about God and about Christ. Compare with Philippians 2:5-11.
4. List the practical problems Paul discussed.

Philemon

Philemon is a letter not to a church but to an individual. It was written at the same time as Colossians. Paul dealt very tactfully here with a difficult problem of personal relations, bringing the question of a returning runaway slave into the light of the Christian fellowship.

Readings

Philemon 1-25.

1. Reconstruct the story behind the letter.
2. Note verse 10 and Colossians 4:9.

Ephesians

Ephesians contains a very general statement of Paul's teaching, not related, as in his letters, to the problems of a specific church. While the letter presents itself as a letter of Paul, a large group of scholars hold that it is not Paul's but was written by a follower or student of Paul.

Readings

Ephesians 1:1-3:13.

1. Study the statements made about Christ.
2. Note that Christianity is for the Greeks. Is the law a pressing problem?

Ephesians 3:14-6:9.

3. List the Christian virtues found here. What is the attitude toward social reform?

Ephesians 6:10-20.

4. Does this reflect a time of persecution?

Ephesians 6:21-24.

5. Compare with Colossians 4:7. If this letter was written by a follower of Paul, which of Paul's letters served as his model?

14

The Gospel and Letters of John

Like the other gospels, the Gospel according to John tells the story of Jesus in order to show what Jesus meant to the church. But in John, the writer's interpretive goal is much more evident to the reader. Here the focus is continually on Jesus as a representative of God and on the question of men's reaction to him. That these are the important things in the story of Jesus is not just implied but made explicit, both by the author's remarks and by the words of Jesus. Jesus, the Son of God, and the need for believing in him—these are the central themes of the fourth gospel.

Thus the view of Christian faith in this gospel has much in common with that of Paul. In contrast to Paul, the long sweep of history, past and future, sinks into the background. The coming of Christ is so tremendously important to the writer that it is the only historical event that matters. In Christ's career God came to men, as He had never come before. The gift of new life which comes to men in Christ is offered to each man, and, if accepted, will transform him into a new kind of person. Christ's coming thus presents each man with a challenge to believe, and a man's fate is decided not at some future judgment, but by his present reaction to the truth that God gives men in Christ.

Like Paul, the author of the fourth gospel continually thought of the presence of Christ's Spirit in the church. When he wrote of the earthly life of Christ, he saw it transfigured by the Christian experience of the Spirit. Unlike Paul, the writer of John was much interested in showing how Christ's work was made effective, not just by his death and resurrection, but by his whole career.

It is probable that John's presentation of the meaning of Christ was worked out in interaction with and opposition to gnosticism. The writer's use of many dualistic terms (light-darkness, above-below, truth-error, etc.), taken with his lack of interest in a future, apocalyptic resolution of the tension between God and evil, suggests that this tradition about Jesus was formulated in tension with gnostic dualism, yet in such a way as to enter into conversation with it. In contrast to the gnostics, this book affirms the central and necessary place of the coming of Christ into human history—the book is a real gospel. At the same time it should be said that the dualistic thought that formed the background of the language of this gospel may well have existed in Judaism. The discovery that much of the language of John has parallels in the Qumran (Dead Sea Scroll) literature has made clear that such language was not necessarily Hellenistic in the sense of being non-Jewish.

In detail, the content of the Gospel according to John is strikingly different from the first three gospels. Most of what they relate was not told by John (though their story is often implied as a background for his). John told a different set of stories and teachings. Where did he get them? The view is still held by some that John's material goes back to a "private" tradition given by Jesus to a few disciples. Most Protestant scholarship, however, holds that while John is based on a tradition of acts and words of Jesus (in part independent of the synoptics), the writer freely rewrote this tradition to bring out more clearly what he believed was its inner meaning. Who this writer was must probably remain an unanswered question. According to ancient church tradition, he was John, son of Zebedee, the disciple of Jesus. But if the gospel represents a reinterpretation of the Christian gospel along the lines suggested above, it is not likely that this John was its author. Though the parallels with Qumran documents have suggested an earlier date to some scholars, the most probable time and place for its writing seems to be not long before 100 A.D. in Ephesus.

Readings

i

John (entire gospel).

1. What does Jesus talk about in this gospel?
2. Where does Jesus work? Note episodes that take place in Jerusalem.
3. Note the miracles recorded by John. How many of these are there?
4. How much ethical teaching is there in this gospel?
5. What parables occur? Are there many proverbial sayings?
6. What is the usual form of Jesus' speech in the Gospel according to John?

ii

John 1:1-18.

1. What is the relation of the Word to creation? to John the Baptist? to Judaism? to the Law? to Jesus? to God?
2. Was the Word present in the world before the life of Jesus? If so, what was its function?
3. What was the function of the Word in the life of Jesus?
4. Compare with Genesis 1:1; Proverbs 8:22-31; Psalm 33:6-9; Isaiah 55:11; Colossians 1:15-17.
5. Why did John think it necessary for the Word to "become flesh"?

iii

John 3:1-21.

1. What is symbolized by Nicodemus' coming at night?
2. "Kingdom of God" occurs only in 3:3-5 in this gospel. Is it present or future?
3. Is Nicodemus' question merely a misunderstanding? Why does he think the new birth impossible?
4. Is water or Spirit more important? What sacrament is related to water?
5. Is the new birth the result of man's initiative?
6. What is the only way to knowledge of heaven, or God's character?

7. Is the death of Jesus regarded as an end or a beginning?
8. What is the point of the comparison with the serpent? (Numbers 21:4-9.)
9. How and when are men judged?
10. What prevents men from believing?
11. What is the result of believing?
12. How is belief brought about?

iv

John 6:1-15.

1. Compare with Mark 6:30-44. Are there any differences in Jesus' part in the story?

John 6:25-51.

2. Are "signs" good or bad? Of what is the feeding of the multitude a sign?
3. Why is the feeding of the multitude an insufficient sign for these questioners?
4. What does Jesus do for men?
5. What power is at work in Jesus? Can this power fail?
6. Why cannot the questioners accept Jesus' statements?
7. When does the new existence imparted by Jesus begin?

John 6:51-59.

8. What Christian sacrament is symbolically connected by these words with the feeding of the multitude?

John 6:60-65.

9. Does the physical aspect of this sacrament greatly interest the author of these words? What aspect of the sacrament does interest him? *Note:* Read John 13 and observe what the author omits from the story of Jesus' last meeting with his disciples as told in Mark 14:12-31.

John 6:66-71.

10. Why can Jesus not prevent the disciples from drawing back?

v

John 9:1-5.

1. What does the healing of the blind man symbolize?
2. What view of suffering is expressed?

John 9:6-34.

3. What different types of reactions to Jesus are found in this section?

John 9:35-41.

4. Why does the former blind man believe?
5. What other result is there of Jesus' activity?
6. Compare with Isaiah 6:9-10.
7. What prevents men from seeing the light? Compare with John 3:16-21.
8. Are those who do not see the light worse off than they were before the coming of Jesus? Why, or why not?

vi

John 10:1-42.

1. What is symbolized by the flock?
2. When did the disciples understand what they could not yet understand in verse 6?
3. What is the reason for the loyalty of the sheep to the shepherd?
4. What is meant by "other sheep, that do not belong to this fold"?
5. How does Jesus' giving his life relate to the "other sheep"?
6. Note verse 24. Has Jesus spoken plainly on this subject? Why is there misunderstanding and doubt?
7. What is the basis of the opposition to Jesus?
8. How does he reply to the objection?

vii

John 12:1-8.

1. Why does Mary pour out the perfume?
2. Why does Jesus accept this "waste"?

John 12:9-19.

3. What did the disciples not understand about this episode at the time?

John 12:20-36.

4. Has this group of inquirers appeared before in the gospel?
5. What was the result of their desire to see Jesus?
6. Why was the coming of this group important to Jesus?

7. What time has come? (See verses 23, 31.)
8. What is the relation between Jesus and his disciples as pictured here?
9. Does Jesus hesitate?
10. What effect will his death have?

John 12:37-50.

11. Does the author believe that man's action is predetermined?
12. Does Jesus offer himself to a selected group or to all?
13. What does Jesus offer to men as he offers himself?

viii

John 13:1-38.

1. Compare with Mark 14:12-31. What meal takes place this night? What does John say in Chapter 6 about the meaning of this meal?
2. What is Jesus trying to show the disciples by his act?
3. Is Judas responsible for what he does?
4. What is the symbolism of night?
5. What guiding principle does Jesus leave with his followers?
6. What is its source?

ix

John 14.

1. What impending event threatens the disciples' readiness to believe in Jesus?
2. What is Jesus' attitude toward this event?
3. How does one enter the "Father's house"?
4. How can one know what God is like?
5. Is the death of Jesus to be the end of his work?
6. Why will Jesus not "show himself to the world"?
7. How will God make Himself known?
8. How are Jesus' life and teachings to live in the group of disciples?
9. How are the disciples to be liberated from fear?
10. Is Jesus afraid of the evil forces in the world?

John 15; 16.

11. What themes recur from Chapter 14? Are any new themes introduced?

John 17.

12. Does Jesus speak as if his work were finished? Why?
13. For whom does he pray? What does he ask for them?

x

John 18; 19.

1. Compare with Mark 14:32-15:47.

John 20; 21.

2. Where do the disciples encounter the risen Lord? Compare with Luke 24 and Matthew 28.
3. Note the author's statement of his purpose (20:30-31).

Read one of the following:

The Interpreter's Bible, Vol. VIII, pp. 437-445.

Kee and Young, *Understanding the New Testament,* pp. 383-414.

Price, *Interpreting the New Testament,* pp. 537-558.

Wright and Fuller, *The Book of the Acts of God,* pp. 379-404.

The Letters of John

The three short letters of John present the same view of the Christian faith as that found in the gospel. Like the gospel, the letters emphasize that Christ came "in human form," that is, that he really participated in human life, and that he is the "only" Son of God, the unique revelation through whom men may know what God is like and receive deliverance from their sins. The writer is deeply concerned that the churches distinguish between true and false Christians. He proposes, in I John, three tests of the real Christian: right belief in Jesus Christ, the Son of God in human form; a real change in moral character; and love—a generous love like that which God has shown in Christ.

Readings

i

I John 1:1-5:21. II John 1-13. III John 1-14.

1. Read the letters of John. Compare the style and the interests of these letters with those of the Gospel according to John.

ii

I John 2:18-25. II John 7-8. III John 9-10.

1. What condition is reflected here?
2. Would this occur early or late in the history of the church?
3. What is the nature of the heresies that the Elder opposes?

iii

I John 1:6-10; 4:1-3; 4:11-21.

1. Note and define the three tests for the genuineness of faith. Are they mentioned elsewhere in the letter?

Read one of the following:

The Interpreter's Bible, Vol. XII, pp. 209-216.

Price, *Interpreting the New Testament,* pp. 530-536.

15

The Catholic and Pastoral Letters and Revelation

Following Paul's letters in the New Testament comes a group of writings known as the "catholic epistles," or general letters; then comes the Christian apocalypse, the book of Revelation. These books are grouped below in accordance with their major interests. Placed with them are the pastoral letters, three letters attributed to Paul, which deal with problems of church organization and belief. The three letters of John, part of the "catholic" group, were placed with his gospel in Chapter 14.[1]

Christian Wisdom Literature

The letter of James is a bit of Christian wisdom, perhaps an ancient sermon. If the author were James, the brother of Jesus, the date of the writing would be within the first Christian generation, but it seems

---

[1] Readings other than the New Testament books themselves have not been noted in this chapter: helpful introductions will be found in Volumes XI and XII of *The Interpreter's Bible* and in appropriate sections of the books we have been citing by Kee and Young, Price, and Wright and Fuller.

probable that the book came somewhat later. In striking contrast to most Christian authors, James showed little interest in stating his view of Christ, but reminiscences of the teaching of Jesus are frequent.

Readings

James 1:1-5:20.

1. What range of topics is discussed?
2. Compare this with the message of Jesus.
3. Notice the attitude toward the rich.
4. Notice the mention of a special group of teachers. Did the author belong to it?
5. Compare the view of faith with that of Paul. (See 2:14-26.)

Literature of Persecution

Three New Testament books deal particularly with the problem of persecution that, though not a constant fact, was a continual threat and occasionally took place with great severity. In addition to official government action, Christians often faced prejudice and discrimination from their neighbors—a kind of "persecution" mentioned in a number of New Testament books. But Revelation, Hebrews, and I Peter deal specifically with real persecution.

Hebrews

Hebrews was long considered to be a letter of Paul, but it is now almost universally considered non-Pauline by Protestant scholars. The central theme of the letter is the excellence and finality of salvation in Christ in comparison with the preliminary sort of salvation found in the Old Testament. For the writer, the Old Testament ritual becomes a foreshadowing of the death of Christ; the old system had tried to bring God and man together, and this was done decisively by Christ. Interwoven with the development of this basic theme is the practical application: stand fast in difficulty and persecution; hold fast to and grow in the faith that you have received. While some would date Hebrews not long after 60 A.D., it seems more probable that it was written late in the first century.

Readings

i

Hebrews 1:1-4; 3:1-6; 5:1-10; 7:1-10:18.

1. In what ways is Christ superior to angels?
2. In what ways is Christ superior to Moses?
3. What is the point of the comparison of Christ and the high priest?
4. Notice the elaborate comparison of Christ's work with the sacrificial system:
   Chapter 7—a better high priest
   Chapter 8—a better sanctuary
   Chapter 9—a better sacrifice
   Chapter 10—summary

ii

Hebrews 10:32-39; 12:1-3; 13:3; 13:12-15.

1. Was the church being persecuted?
2. Was it their first experience of persecution?
3. Was the author sure that they would stand up under persecution?

iii

Hebrews 2:1-4; 3:7-4:3; 12:12.

1. What danger was the author trying to combat here?

iv

Hebrews 10:19-31.

1. State the doctrine presented here.

Hebrews 12:18-29.

2. To what emotion does this passage appeal?

v

Hebrews 11:1-40.

1. What does "faith" mean to the writer? Compare with Paul.
2. What was the practical application of the chapter? Note how it connects with Chapter 12.

vi

Hebrews 5:11-6:8.

1. State the challenge you find here. Some hold that I Peter was a response to this challenge.

I Peter

I Peter encourages Christians who face severe trials, both social discrimination and outright persecution. The author's emphasis on submission to the authorities, as to agents of God's will, shows that his attitude toward Rome is like that of Paul rather than that of the book of Revelation. A prominent theme throughout the book is the value of submission and suffering, which bring the believer closer to Christ. The letter is directed to Christians in Asia Minor. As to date and authorship there is wide difference of opinion. Many hold that the apostle Peter was the author, in which case the date would be about 60 A.D. Others find that the letter better fits the situation of the church in the late first century.

Readings

i

I Peter 1:1-5:14.

1. Read I Peter and note the main themes of the letter.

ii

I Peter 1:1-2; 5:13.

1. To whom is the letter addressed?
2. Note the place of writing. Was the letter written in Babylon? What else could "Babylon" mean? (See Revelation 18.)

iii

I Peter 2:13-17; 3:8-4:6.

1. Do these passages show the same spirit as Revelation 18:4-20?
2. Do they try to counteract this spirit?

iv

I Peter 2:13-3:7.

1. What kind of action is especially stressed?
2. Does the author discuss the responsibility of those in authority?

v

I Peter 2:11-12; 4:7-11.

1. What did the author mean by "exiles"?

vi

I Peter 4:12-19.

1. What is the setting?

Revelation

Revelation is a Christian apocalypse. Its thought is closely related to that of the book of Daniel, though in Revelation the fulfillment of God's purpose is to be accomplished by Christ. Like Daniel, the practical purpose of the book is to encourage firm endurance; like Daniel too, the book concentrates on the wonderful future that lies ahead for God's people (the church). As for the world, only destruction and punishment are to be its future. The symbolic language of the book is forceful and poetic, but its obscurity has made Revelation a favorite source for peculiar interpretations of the Christian religion. The book is usually dated about 96 A.D. and connected with a persecution of Christians by the Emperor Domitian at that time.

Readings

i

Read the book of Revelation.

1. Notice the alternation of woes on earth and peace in heaven. What is the effect on the reader of this contrast?
2. Is the final triumph expected soon?

3. What attitude does the book show toward the opponents of the church?
4. What reaction does the book encourage in the faithful?
5. Note the sections in the book in which there are direct references to Christ. Are these sections many?

ii

Revelation 1:1-3:22.

1. Notice the series of letters. What collection of New Testament letters might have suggested this form, if it was already in circulation?
2. What virtues do the letters especially praise?
3. What situation in the church do they reflect?

iii

Revelation 4:1-5:14.

1. Compare with Ezekiel's vision (Ezekiel 1:1-2:8).

Revelation 10:8-11.

2. Compare with Ezekiel 2:8-3:15.

Revelation 13:1-18.

3. Compare with Daniel 7.

Revelation 5:1.

4. Note exactly what the writer sees. Could one see both sides of a sealed scroll?
5. Do these visions appear to be direct visions or imaginative literary creations based on earlier tradition?

iv

Revelation 6:1-17; 8:1-9:21; 11:14-19; 12:1-13:18; 15:1-20:3.

1. Notice the three series of seven catastrophes and the final victory over the power of evil.
2. Are these historical catastrophes, as in Amos and Jeremiah? If not, how would you describe them?
3. In what form is the power of evil concentrated? (Note especially Revelation 17:18; 18:10-24.) Compare with the book of Daniel.

v

Revelation 7:1-17; 10:1-11:19; 14:1-20.

1. What is the theme of these sections?

vi

Revelation 20:4-10.

1. Here is the only reference in the Bible to the thousand-year reign of Christ and the "saints" on earth. Does it have any relation to the prophetic hope for a triumph of God's will on earth?

Revelation 20:11-15.

2. Where has this theme been most directly presented in other biblical books?

Revelation 21:1-22:21.

3. Why is the final triumph of God presented as a city?

Literature of Organization and Consolidation

Early in the second century a corpus of three letters was written to combat the heresies that had arisen and to deal with problems of the organization of the church. They were written as though from Paul to his friends Timothy and Titus and may contain portions of letters written by Paul. These letters, I and II Timothy and Titus, are known as the "pastoral epistles" because of their interest in the problems of church leadership.

Jude and II Peter, also writings of the second century, are likewise largely concerned with opposing heresy.

The Pastoral Letters
(I and II Timothy and Titus)

i

I Timothy 1:1-6:21. II Timothy 1:1-4:22. Titus 1:1-3:15.

1. Read the pastoral letters. Note the sections that deal with problems of church leadership, moral behavior, and belief.

ii

I Timothy 6:3-6; 6:20-21. II Timothy 2:14-26; 3:12-17.
Titus 1:10-2:14.

1. What conditions in the church are reflected here?
2. What specific heresies are attacked?
3. What motives does the author attribute to the heretics?

iii

II Timothy 2:14-17. Titus 3:8-11.

1. Has the tendency Paul decried in I Corinthians 12 decreased?
2. Is the problem different from Paul's?

iv

I Timothy 3:1-13; 5:17-25.

1. What offices are mentioned here?
2. Were there professional officers at this time?
3. By what practical means did the author try to combat heresy and schism?

Jude

Jude 1-25.

1. What practices and ideas was the author rebuking?
2. On what basis?

II Peter

i

II Peter 1:1-3:18.

1. Note how all of the book of Jude is incorporated in paraphrase.
2. What problem other than the problem of Jude is discussed?

ii

II Peter 3:15-16.

1. What status did Paul's letters have when this epistle was written?

Supplementary Materials

The Canon

The history of the canon is difficult to outline. Dates of "canonization" usually mean dates of "closing" the canon. In fact, books cannot be canonized by the fiat of a council. The books that grow in the influence they have in the practice of worship and over the lives of men, generation after generation, become revered. A book becomes sacred by the same sort of process through which another becomes a classic. Experience gleans the more valuable books from the less valuable, and these become recognized as inspiring and authoritative. The final act of canonization is always a matter of confirming the judgment of experience and closing the list to books that have not measured up. At times artificial rules have guided this final act and books of lesser value have been accepted. But even this does not make these lesser books greater. The only final sanction is found in the minds and hearts of men. The lesser books are canonized but not read.

Josiah "canonized" a book of law in 621 B.C. This was the law of Moses as his generation knew it. Ezra-Nehemiah canonized the Law about 450 B.C. Again, this was the ancient Law as they knew it in their day. The book was new, but the Law was ancient.

How the Prophets were canonized we can only guess. But Sirach knew them as a part of the canon early in the second century B.C., and Jesus spoke of "the Law and the Prophets" whenever he spoke of Scripture. Yet Jesus quoted the Psalms as though all recognized them, too, as authoritative.

The Council of Jamnia in 91 A.D. confirmed the admission of the Writings and closed the Jewish canon for Palestinian Jews. But the Jews of Alexandria had had their Bible in Greek for three hundred years (the Septuagint), and by the time the Septuagint came to be used by Christians it contained fourteen books or parts of books not found in the Hebrew Scriptures.

Just how the Greek-speaking Jews regarded these added books is not certain, but the Greek Old Testament became the canonical standard for Greek-speaking Christians. Jerome included the whole Greek Old Testament in his Latin Vulgate in accordance with the custom of the time, though he regarded the books found only in the Septuagint as of inferior value. He gave currency to the term "Apocrypha" as a name for them.

Meanwhile Christianity had produced books that gradually climbed to a position beside the Scripture. The gospels and the letters of Paul formed the core of the new collection. By 200 A.D., the gospels, Acts, Paul's letters, and many of the catholic letters were revered by Christians everywhere. But Revelation and some other books were sometimes omitted, while many Christian groups included books later dropped from the canon. The New Testament canon has been fixed for the western church since the Council of Carthage (396 A.D.).

Protestantism gradually dropped the Apocrypha from the canon. Luther's German Bible pulled these books out of place and lumped them together. English printed Bibles followed this example, placing them between the Old and New Testaments. Gradually they were dropped entirely. For Roman Catholics they are part of the canon and are not grouped in a separate collection.

The Law
(Torah) (Pentateuch)
Genesis, Exodus, Leviticus, Numbers, Deuteronomy.

The Prophets (Nebiim)

Former Prophets: Joshua, Judges, Samuel (I and II), Kings (I and II).

Latter Prophets: Isaiah, Jeremiah, Ezekiel, and "The Twelve."

The Twelve: Hosea, Joel, Amos, Obadiah, Jonah, Micah, Nahum, Habakkuk, Zephaniah, Haggai, Zachariah, Malachi.

The Writings (Hagiographa)
(Kethubim)

Psalms, Job, Proverbs, Ruth, Song of Songs, Ecclesiastes, Lamentations, Esther, Daniel, Ezra, Nehemiah, Chronicles (I and II).

The Apocrypha

Esdras (I and II),[1] Tobit, Judith, some additions to Esther, Wisdom of Solomon, Ecclesiasticus (Wisdom of Sirach), Baruch, Susanna, Song of the Three Children, Bel and the Dragon, Prayer of Manasseh, Maccabees (I and II).

The New Testament

Matthew, Mark, Luke, John, Acts, Romans, Corinthians (I and II), Galatians, Ephesians, Philippians, Colossians, Thessalonians (I and II), Timothy (I and II), Titus, Philemon, Hebrews, James, Peter (I and II), John (I, II, and III), Jude, Revelation.

[1] The Vulgate's I, II, III, and IV Esdras are Ezra, Nehemiah, I and II Esdras in the Protestant Bible and Apocrypha.

The Apocrypha

The Apocrypha are Jewish writings that came to the Christian Church in the Greek Old Testament. For the place of the Apocrypha in the Christian canon, see above, p. 172. In the following sketch neither the original languages nor the dates can be fixed with accuracy in every case, but the writings are arranged in approximate chronological order.

200 B.C.	*Tobit* (Hebrew or Aramaic). A short novel that teaches Jewish religion and morality.
180 B.C. (130 B.C.)	*Ecclesiasticus* (Hebrew). The proverbial wisdom of Jeshua, the son of Sirach, written in Palestine about 180; Greek translation by his grandson, in Egypt about 130 B.C.
150 B.C.	*The Song of the Three Children* and the *Prayer of Azarias* (Hebrew). "Psalms" added to the Book of Daniel.

150 B.C.   *I Esdras*. A fragment of a Greek translation of Chronicles-Ezra-Nehemiah, within which has been inserted a popular oriental tale.

150 B.C.   *Judith* (Hebrew). A hero tale emphasizing nationalism (like Esther), and the observance of the law.

100 B.C.   *Prayer of Manasseh* (? Hebrew). Written to follow II Chronicles 33:19. A prayer of repentance.

100 B.C.   *Additions to Esther* (various). Inserted into the book to modify it in various ways.

100 B.C.   *Additions to Daniel—Susanna* (? Hebrew). A popular oriental tale used to point toward sound legal practice. *Bel and the Dragon* (? Hebrew). Popular stories that ridicule idolatry.

100 B.C.   *I Maccabees* (Hebrew). A careful and patriotic history of the Maccabean struggle against Syria.

100 B.C.   *II Maccabees* (Greek). A romanticized history of the Maccabean struggle covering much of the same ground as I Maccabees. An abridgment of a longer work now lost.

100 B.C.   *Wisdom of Solomon* (? Greek). A book of wisdom showing Greek influence.

100 B.C.   *Baruch* (? Hebrew). A composite book attributed to the secretary of Jeremiah; combines "prophecy" and "wisdom." Sometimes dated after 70 A.D., in which case it would serve to encourage the Jews after the fall of Jerusalem. *Baruch, Chapter 6—The Letter of Jeremiah* (? Greek). An attack on idolatry.

100 A.D.   *II Esdras* (? Aramaic). A Jewish apocalypse inspired by the fall of Jerusalem containing profound reflections on the problem of evil. Not now extant in Greek, but found in the Latin Vulgate.

The Flood Stories

The biblical flood story is a good example of the close connection between biblical stories and older traditions of the area and the way in which two documents were woven together. In the following section, the biblical story of the flood is separated into two continuous stories, one the J story of the flood, the other the P story. As noted above, in the section on the documentary theory (pp. 82-85), this kind of separation is hypothetical and based entirely on internal evidence; that is, differences within the story found in the Bible. However, the flood story affords a rather clear-cut case of the interweaving of two versions of the same story. In many parts of the Pentateuch it is not possible to separate the various documents so clearly. Of course since two overlapping stories have been woven together, according to the documentary theory, parts of both may well have been omitted and other parts rearranged, so that the two stories of the flood below do not represent exactly what stood in the original versions before they were interwoven.

Following the two biblical stories is an abridged version of the Babylonian story of the flood, for comparison.

Although students would differ on details, the following separation of Genesis 6-9 into two versions makes clear the kind of interweaving of sources that the documentary theory presupposes. The sources for the J and P stories are as follows:

J Genesis 6:5-8
   Genesis 7:1-5, 7-10, 12, 16b, 17b, 22-23
   Genesis 8:2b-3a, 6-12, 13b, 20-22
P Genesis 6:9-22
   Genesis 7:6, 11, 13-16a, 17a, 18-21, 24
   Genesis 8:1-2a, 3b-5, 13a, 14-19
   Genesis 9:1-17.

Read the following attempts to separate the J and P stories of the flood, and the Babylonian story of the flood, then answer these questions:[1]

1. Note the differences in style between J and P.
2. How many pairs of animals were in the ark according to J and P?
3. How long did the flood last according to J and P?
4. According to the J version, what made it necessary to have more than one pair of clean animals?
5. Does the P version recognize a system of "clean" and "unclean" animals in Noah's day?
6. Note parallels to Genesis 1:27, Leviticus 17:10-14, and Numbers 35 in the P version.
7. Compare the Hebrew and Babylonian flood stories.
8. What was the reason for the flood in the Babylonian story?

The J Story of the Flood [1]

When the Lord saw that the wickedness of man on the earth was great, and that the whole bent of his thinking was never of anything

[1] The flood story as here presented is a rearrangement of the Smith-Goodspeed translation. Reprinted from *The Bible: An American Translation*, trans. by J. M. P. Smith, Edgar J. Goodspeed, and others, by permission of the University of Chicago Press. Copyright 1923, 1927, 1948 by the University of Chicago.

but evil, the Lord regretted that he had ever made man on the earth, and he was grieved to the heart. So the Lord said, "I will blot the men that I have created off the face of the ground, both men and animals, reptiles, and birds of the air; for I regret that I ever made them." Noah, however, had found favor with the Lord.

The Lord said to Noah,

> Enter the ark, with all your household; for you alone of the present age have I found righteous. Of all clean animals, you are to take seven pairs, a male with its mate; but of all the animals that are not clean a pair, a male with its mate; likewise, of the birds of the air seven pairs, a male and a female—to keep their kind alive all over the earth. For in seven days' time I am going to make it rain for forty days and nights on the earth, to blot off the face of the earth every living thing that I have made.

Noah did just as God had commanded him. Noah, with his sons, his wife, and his sons' wives, went into the ark to escape the waters of the flood. Of the clean animals and of those that were not clean, of the birds, and of all the reptiles, a pair of each, a male and a female, joined Noah in the ark, as God had commanded Noah. Then, at the end of the seven days the waters of the flood came on the earth. (The rain fell on the earth for forty days and nights.) Then the Lord shut him in. The waters mounted, and lifted the ark so that it rose above the earth. Of all that was on the land, everything in whose nostrils was the breath of life died; every living thing was blotted off the face of the earth, both men and animals and reptiles and birds; they were blotted off the earth, so that Noah alone was left, and those that were with him in the ark.

The rain from the heavens ceased, and the waters abated steadily from the earth. At the end of forty days Noah opened the window that he made in the ark, and released a raven, which went flying back and forth until the waters had dried off the earth. Then he released a dove, to see whether the waters had subsided from the surface of the land; but the dove could find no resting-place for the sole of her foot, so she came back to him into the ark; for there was water all over the earth. He put out his hand, and catching her, drew her into the ark with him. After waiting another seven days, he again released the dove from the ark; in the evening the dove came back to him, and there, in her beak, was a freshly-picked olive leaf! So Noah knew that the waters had subsided off the earth. After waiting another seven days, he released the dove, but she never came back to him. So Noah removed the covering of the ark and found that the surface of the ground was quite dry.

Then Noah built an altar to the Lord, and taking some clean animals and birds of every kind, he offered them as burnt-offerings on the altar. When the Lord smelled the soothing odor, the Lord said to himself,

> I will never again curse the soil because of man, though the bent of man's mind may be evil from his very youth; nor will I ever again destroy all life, as I have just done. As long as the earth endures, seedtime and harvest, cold and heat, summer and winter, day and night, shall never cease.

The P Story of the Flood

The following are the descendants of Noah. Noah alone among his contemporaries was a pious and exceedingly good man; Noah walked with God. Noah had three sons born to him, Shem, Ham, and Japheth. Now in God's sight, the earth was corrupt; the earth was full of wrong-doing; God saw that the earth was corrupt; for every mortal man on earth corrupted his life. So God said to Noah,

> I have resolved on the extermination of all mortals; for the earth is full of wrong-doing through them; I am going to exterminate them from the earth. Make yourself an ark of oleander wood; make the ark with cabins, and smear it with bitumen inside and out. This is how you are to make it: the length of the ark is to be three hundred cubits, its breadth fifty cubits, and its height thirty cubits; you are to make a roof for the ark, finishing it off on top to the width of a cubit; and the doorway of the ark you are to put in its side; you are to make it with lower, second, and third decks. I on my part am about to bring a flood upon the earth, to destroy every mortal man from under the heavens, who has the breath of life in him; everything that is on the earth shall perish. But with you I will make a covenant; you shall enter the ark, accompanied by your sons, your wife, and your sons' wives. Also, of all living creatures, of all animals, you must have two of every kind enter the ark, to keep them alive with you; they are to be a male and a female. Of the various kinds of birds, the various kinds of animals, and all the various kinds of reptiles, two of every kind are to join you, that you may keep them alive. Take also some of every kind of edible food, and store it by you, to be food for yourself and them.

Noah did so; he did just as God had commanded him. Noah was six hundred years old when the flood came on the earth. In the six hundredth year of Noah's life, on the seventeenth day of the second month, on that very day the foundations of the great abyss were all broken open, and the windows of the heavens were opened. That same day Noah, with Shem, Ham, and Japheth, Noah's sons, and Noah's wife, and the three wives of his sons accompanying them, went into the ark, together with all the various kinds of wild beasts, all the various kinds of domestic animals, all the various kinds of land reptiles, and all the various kinds of birds, everything with feathers and wings; of all creatures in which there was the breath of life, a pair of each joined Noah in the ark. Those that entered were a male and a female of every kind of animal, as God had commanded him. The flood continued for forty days upon the earth. The waters rose and increased greatly on the earth, so that the ark floated on the surface of the waters. The waters rose higher and higher on the earth, until the highest mountains everywhere under the heavens were all covered. Fifteen cubits above them the waters rose, so that the mountains were covered. Every creature that moved on the earth perished, including birds, domestic animals, wild beasts, all the land reptiles, and all mankind. The waters rose on the earth for one hundred and fifty days.

Then God remembered Noah, and all the wild and domestic animals that were with him in the ark; so God made a wind blow over the earth, and the waters subsided. Likewise, the fountains of the abyss and the windows of the heavens were closed. At the end of one hundred and fifty days the water subsided, so that on the seventeenth day of the seventh month the ark grounded on the mountains of Ararat. The waters subsided steadily until the tenth month; and on the first day of the tenth month the tops of the mountains became visible. By the first day of the first month of the six hundred and first year of Noah's life the waters had dried off the earth. By the twenty-seventh day of the second month the earth was dry.

Then God said to Noah,

Come out of the ark, your wife, your sons, and your sons' wives accompanying you; bring out with you every animal of every sort that is with you, birds, quadrupeds, and all land reptiles, that they may breed freely on the earth, and be fruitful and multiply on the earth.

So Noah came out, his sons, his wife, and his sons' wives accompanying him. Every animal, every reptile, and every bird, everything that moves on the earth came out of the ark by their species. God blessed Noah and his sons, and said to them.

Be fruitful, multiply, and fill the earth. The fear and dread of you shall be on every wild beast of the earth and on every bird of the air; as in the case of all the reptiles on the ground and all the fish of the sea, they have been delivered into your power. Everything that moves, that is alive, is to be food for you; as I once gave you the green plants, I now give you everything. Only, you must never eat flesh with the life (that is, the blood) in it. For your own life-blood, however, I will require an account; I will hold every animal accountable for it, and I will hold men accountable for one another's lives; whoever sheds the blood of man, by man shall his blood be shed; for God made man in his own image. As for you, then, be fruitful, and multiply; be prolific in the earth and multiply in it.

God then said to Noah and to his sons with him,

As for me, I do herewith establish my covenant with you and your descendants after you, and with every living creature that is with you, the birds, the domestic animals, and all the wild beasts with you, as many of them as came out of the ark; I establish my covenant with you, that never again shall all flesh be destroyed by the waters of a flood, and never again shall there be a flood to ravage the earth.

Further, God said,

This shall be the symbol of the covenant which I am making between myself and you and every living creature that is with you, to endless generations: I put my rainbow in the clouds, and it shall be a symbol of the covenant between myself and the world. Whenever I bring clouds over the earth, the rainbow will appear in the clouds, and then I will remember my covenant, which obtains between myself and you and every living creature of every sort, and the waters shall never again become a flood to destroy all flesh. When the rainbow appears in the clouds, I will see it, and remember the everlasting covenant between God and every living creature of every sort that is on the earth.

God said to Noah,

This shall be the symbol of the covenant which I am making between myself and all flesh that is on the earth.

The Babylonian Story of the Flood

The close relation between the biblical story, or stories, of the flood and the Babylonian story has long been recognized. The Babylonian story appears in various versions and is clearly an ancient and widespread tale. It is best preserved in the Gilgamesh Epic, the story of a hero who seeks (without success) to find immortality. In the quest he goes to Utnapishtim, a man who long before had survived the flood and afterward been made immortal. Utnapishtim tells the story of the flood to Gilgamesh. The fullest written account of the Gilgamesh Epic comes from the seventh century B.C., but the story was composed perhaps as early as 2000 B.C., and the flood story, originally separate, is probably older still. Here Utnapishtim's story is presented in abridged form from the full version of E. A. Speiser in *Ancient Near Eastern Texts Relating to the Old Testament,* pp. 93-95.[1] The story, preserved on clay tablets, is somewhat fragmentary, and some words have been restored that are missing in the original text.

> Utnapishtim said to him, to Gilgamesh:
> "I will reveal to thee, Gilgamesh, a hidden matter
> And a secret of the gods will I tell thee:
> Shurippak—a city which thou knowest,
> And which on Euphrates' banks is situate—
> That city was ancient, as were the gods within it,
> When their heart led the great gods to produce the flood.
> There were Anu, their father,
> Valiant Enlil, their counselor,
> Ninurta, their herald,
> Ennuge, their foreman.
> Ninigiku-Ea was also present with them;
> Their words he repeats to the reed-hut:[2] . . .
> 'Man of Shuruppak, son of Ubar-Tutu,
> Tear down this house, build a ship!
> Give up possessions, seek thou life.
> Forswear possessions and keep the soul alive!
> Aboard the ship take thou the seed of all living things.
> The ship that thou shalt build,

---

[1] Edited by James B. Pritchard (Princeton: Princeton University Press, copyright 1950; rev. ed. 1955). Reprinted by permission.
[2] The god Ea speaks to Utnapishtim, who is within the hut.

Her dimensions shall be to measure.
Equal shall be her width and her length' . . .
    [The god Ea, who has just revealed to Utnapishtim the plan of the
gods to destroy life by the flood, now tells Utnapishtim how to de-
ceive the citizens of Shuruppak so that they will not suspect what
is going to happen. Utnapishtim leads them to think that he is
preparing to flee from the hatred of the god Enlil; the citizens
help in the building of the ship.]
On the fifth day I laid her framework.
One whole acre was her floor space,
    Ten dozen cubits the height of each of her walls,
Ten dozen cubits each edge of the square deck.
I laid out her contours and joined her together.
I provided her with six decks,
Dividing her thus into seven parts. . . .
Six sar (measures) of bitumen I poured into the furnace,
Three sar of asphalt I also poured inside. . . .
On the seventh day the ship was completed. . . .
All my family and kin I made go aboard the ship,
The beasts of the field, the wild creatures of the field,
    All the craftsmen I made go aboard.
Shamash had set for me a stated time:
'When he who orders unease at night,
    Will shower down a rain of blight,
Board thou the ship and batten up the gate.'
That stated time had arrived:
'He who orders unease at night, showers down a rain of blight.'
I watched the appearance of the weather.
The weather was awesome to behold.
I boarded the ship and battened up the gate. . . .
With the first glow of dawn,
A black cloud rose up from the horizon.
Inside it Adad thunders,
While Shullat and Hanish go in front, . . .
Consternation over Adad reaches to the heavens,
Turning to blackness all that had been light.
The wide land was shattered like a pot!
For one day the south-storm blew,
Gathering speed as it blew, submerging the mountains,
Overtaking the people like a battle.
No one can see his fellow,
Nor can the people be recognized from heaven.
The gods were frightened by the deluge,
And, shrinking back, they ascended to the heaven of Anu.
The gods cowered like dogs
    Crouched against the outer wall. . . .

[Omitted here is a section which gives the lament of the gods.]

The gods, all humbled, sit and weep,
Their lips drawn tight, . . . one and all.
Six days and six nights
Blows the flood wind, as the south-storm sweeps the land.
When the seventh day arrived,
   The flood-carrying south-storm subsided in the battle,
Which it had fought like an army.
The sea grew quiet, the tempest was still, the flood ceased.
I looked at the weather: stillness had set in.
And all of mankind had returned to clay.
The landscape was as level as a flat roof.
I opened a hatch, and light fell upon my face.
Bowing low, I sat and wept,
Tears running down my face.
I looked about for coast lines in the expanse of the sea:
In each of fourteen regions
   There emerged a region-mountain.
On Mount Nisir the ship came to a halt.
Mount Nisir held the ship fast,
   Allowing no motion.
One day, a second day, Mount Nisir held the ship fast,
   Allowing no motion. . . .
When the seventh day arrived,
I sent forth and set free a dove.
The dove went forth, but came back;
Since no resting-place for it was visible she turned round.
Then I sent forth and set free a swallow.
The swallow went forth, but came back;
Since no resting-place for it was visible she turned round.
Then I sent forth and set free a raven.
The raven went forth and, seeing that the waters had diminished,
He eats, circles, caws, and turns not round.
Then I let out all to the four winds
   And offered a sacrifice.
I poured out a libation on the top of the mountain,
Seven and seven cult-vessels I set up,
Upon their pot-stands I heaped cane, cedarwood, and myrtle.
The gods smelled the savor,
The gods smelled the sweet savor,
The gods crowded like flies about the sacrificer.
When at length the great goddess arrived,
She lifted up the great jewels which Anu had fashioned to her liking:
'Ye gods, as surely as this lapis
   Upon my neck I shall not forget,
I shall be mindful of these days, forgetting them never.
Let the gods come to the offering;

But let not Enlil come to the offering,
For he, unreasoning, brought on the deluge
And my people consigned to destruction.'
When at length Enlil arrived,
And saw the ship, Enlil was wroth,
He was filled with wrath over the Igigi gods:[1]
'Has some living soul escaped?
    No man was to survive the destruction!' . . .
Ea opened his mouth to speak,
    Saying to valiant Enlil:
'Thou wisest of gods, thou hero,
How couldst thou, unreasoning, bring on the deluge?
On the sinner impose his sin,
    On the transgressor impose his transgression!
Yet be lenient, lest he be cut off,
Be patient, lest he be dislodged!
Instead of thy bringing on the deluge,
    Would that a lion had risen up to diminish mankind!
Instead of thy bringing on the deluge,
    Would that a wolf had risen up to diminish mankind! . . .
It was not I who disclosed the secret of the great gods.
I let Atrahasis[2] see a dream,
    And he perceived the secret of the gods.
Now then take counsel in regard to him!'
Thereupon Enlil went aboard the ship.
Holding me by the hand, he took me aboard.
He took my wife aboard and made her kneel by my side.
Standing between us, he touched our foreheads to bless us:
'Hitherto Utnapishtim has been but human.
Henceforth Utnapishtim and his wife shall be like unto us gods.
Utnapishtim shall reside far away, at the mouth of the rivers!'
Thus they took me and made me reside far away,
    At the mouth of the rivers."

[1] The heavenly gods.
[2] A name for Utnapishtim.

OUTLINE OF
BIBLICAL HISTORY

Scale |————————————| = *100 Years*

LITERATURE	DATES AND PERIODS	PERSONS AND EVENTS
	1400 B.C.	
	Virtually all dates for literature are approximate; also other dates before eighth century B.C.	*Perhaps as early as the fifteenth century, probably in the fourteenth or early thirteenth, the Hebrew slaves escaped from Egypt.*
	1300 B.C.	
The literature of the early years was composed and transmitted orally.	EXODUS WANDERING	MOSES • Covenant with Yahweh
It consisted of: STORIES LAWS POEMS SONGS *such as the Song of Deborah (Judges 5)*	CONQUEST 1200 B.C.	• The conquest of Palestine was gradual; frequent fights; constant intermarry- JOSHUA ing; infiltrating, forming alliances.
		THE "JUDGES" *As the Hebrews shifted from nomadic to agricultural life, Canaanite culture and religion filtered into their lives.*
	1100 B.C.	

185

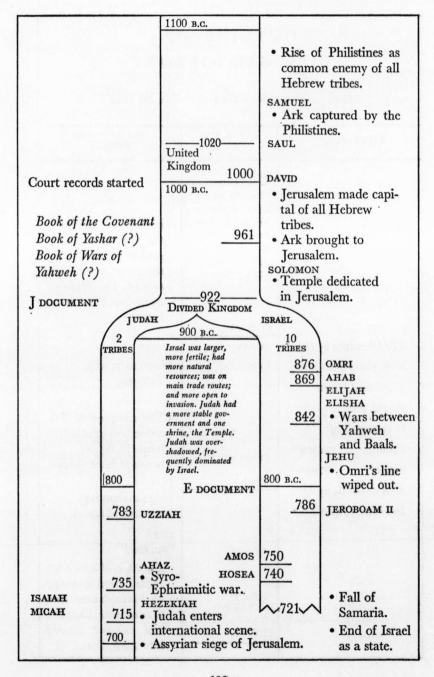

1100 B.C.

Court records started

Book of the Covenant
Book of Yashar (?)
Book of Wars of
Yahweh (?)

J DOCUMENT

- Rise of Philistines as common enemy of all Hebrew tribes.

SAMUEL
- Ark captured by the Philistines.

SAUL

——1020——
United Kingdom 1000

1000 B.C.

DAVID
- Jerusalem made capital of all Hebrew tribes.
- Ark brought to Jerusalem.

SOLOMON
- Temple dedicated in Jerusalem.

961

——922——
DIVIDED KINGDOM

JUDAH   ISRAEL

2 TRIBES   900 B.C.   10 TRIBES

Israel was larger, more fertile; had more natural resources; was on main trade routes; and more open to invasion. Judah had a more stable government and one shrine, the Temple. Judah was overshadowed, frequently dominated by Israel.

876 OMRI
869 AHAB
ELIJAH
ELISHA
842
- Wars between Yahweh and Baals.

JEHU
- Omri's line wiped out.

800   E DOCUMENT   800 B.C.

786 JEROBOAM II

783 UZZIAH

ISAIAH
MICAH

AMOS 750
HOSEA 740

AHAZ
735
- Syro-Ephraimitic war.

HEZEKIAH
715
- Judah enters international scene.

721
- Fall of Samaria.
- End of Israel as a state.

700
- Assyrian siege of Jerusalem.

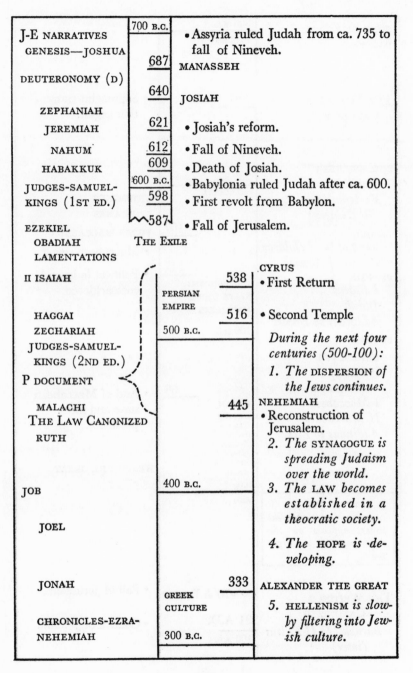

	700 B.C.	• Assyria ruled Judah from ca. 735 to fall of Nineveh.
J-E NARRATIVES GENESIS—JOSHUA		
	687	MANASSEH
DEUTERONOMY (D)		
	640	JOSIAH
ZEPHANIAH		
JEREMIAH	621	• Josiah's reform.
NAHUM	612	• Fall of Nineveh.
HABAKKUK	609	• Death of Josiah.
JUDGES-SAMUEL- KINGS (1ST ED.)	600 B.C.	• Babylonia ruled Judah after ca. 600.
	598	• First revolt from Babylon.
	587	• Fall of Jerusalem.
EZEKIEL OBADIAH LAMENTATIONS	THE EXILE	
II ISAIAH	538	CYRUS • First Return
	PERSIAN EMPIRE	
HAGGAI ZECHARIAH	516	• Second Temple
	500 B.C.	*During the next four centuries (500-100):*
JUDGES-SAMUEL- KINGS (2ND ED.)		*1. The* DISPERSION *of the Jews continues.*
P DOCUMENT		
MALACHI THE LAW CANONIZED	445	NEHEMIAH • Reconstruction of Jerusalem.
RUTH		*2. The* SYNAGOGUE *is spreading Judaism over the world.*
	400 B.C.	*3. The* LAW *becomes established in a theocratic society.*
JOB		
JOEL		*4. The* HOPE *is ·developing.*
JONAH	333	ALEXANDER THE GREAT
	GREEK CULTURE	*5.* HELLENISM *is slowly filtering into Jewish culture.*
CHRONICLES-EZRA- NEHEMIAH	300 B.C.	

187

	300 B.C.	
SONG OF SONGS PROVERBS	PTOLEMIES	
THE PROPHETS CANONIZED	250	• Septuagint translation begun.
ECCLESIASTES *Tobit* *Ecclesiasticus* *(in Hebrew)*	200 B.C. SELEUCIDS	ANTIOCHUS EPIPHANES
DANIEL *Song of the 3 children* *Prayer of Azarias*	167	JUDAS MACCABEUS • Maccabean revolt.
PSALMS *I Esdras* *Judith* *Additions to Daniel*	142 INDEPENDENT STATE UNDER MACCABEES 100 B.C.	• Political independence achieved.
ESTHER *Baruch (?)* *Prayer of* *Manasseh* *I Maccabees* *II Maccabees* *Additions to Esther*	63 ROMAN EMPIRE	• End of Maccabean state and independence.
Wisdom of *Solomon*	B.C.	HEROD THE GREAT
A chart of this period, covering New Testament times, appears on the next page on a larger scale.	A.D.	
THE WRITINGS CANONIZED	∿70 A.D.∿	• Fall of Jerusalem.
Baruch (?) II Esdras *(later)*	91 A.D. 100 A.D.	• Council of Jamnia.

NEW TESTAMENT TIMES

Scale |—————————| = *50 Years*

'ROMAN EMPIRE

6 B.C. • Birth of Jesus.

4 B.C. •Death of Herod the

B.C. Great.

A.D.

JESUS

30 • Crucifixion.

Galatians
I II Thessalonians   50 A.D.   PAUL
I II Corinthians
Romans, Philippians   •Rise of the
Colossians, Philemon   Christian church.

MARK   70   • Fall of Jerusalem.

MATTHEW

LUKE-ACTS *Ephesians,*
Hebrews,   91   •Council of Jamnia.
Revelation,
I Peter, James
JOHN   100 A.D.
I II III John

Jude
I II Timothy
Titus

II Peter   150 A.D.

Bibliography

This bibliography suggests only a few of the books that can guide the student of the Bible. Of the many guides to further reading, perhaps the most useful are the bibliographies in the various sections of the *Interpreter's Bible* and at the end of the articles in the *Interpreter's Dictionary*. The books listed below include both surveys and creative scholarly works, both of which are useful even for the beginning student.

Books marked with an asterisk (*) are those from which the suggested readings are taken.

I. Translations of the Bible

The Bible: An American Translation, J. M. P. Smith and Edgar J. Goodspeed, eds. Chicago: The University of Chicago Press, 1948. The most useful of the modern speech translations. A translation into simple American speech.

The Holy Bible. Revised Standard Version. New York: Thomas Nelson & Sons, 1952. A thorough revision of the traditional translation, making it both more accurate and more readable.

The Oxford Annotated Bible, Herbert G. May and Bruce M. Metzger, eds. New York: Oxford University Press, 1962. The Revised Standard Version with useful introductions and notes.

190

II. The Approach to the Bible

Brown, Robert McAfee, *The Bible Speaks to You.* Philadelphia: Westminster Press, 1955. A statement in fresh, colloquial style of the impact of the Bible on the modern inquirer.

* Dodd, C. H., *The Bible Today.* London: Cambridge University Press, 1960. A stimulating discussion of how the Bible is to be studied, what it contains, and how it bears on the life of man today.

Richardson, Alan, *A Preface to Bible Study.* Philadelphia: Westminster Press, 1954. A thoughtful introduction to study in the context of the Christian faith.

III. The History of the Bible

Bruce, F. F., *The English Bible.* New York: Oxford University Press, 1961. A thorough and interesting history of the English translations.

Price, Ira M., *The Ancestry of Our English Bible,* 2nd. ed. Revised by William A. Irwin and Allen Wikgren. New York: Harper & Row, Publishers, 1949. A good survey of the ancient history of the Bible and its various versions, as well as a study of the history of the English Bible.

IV. Old Testament History and Faith

* Albright, William F., *The Biblical Period from Abraham to Ezra.* New York: Harper Torchbooks, 1963. A concise and brilliant sketch of Hebrew history making use of the findings of archaeological study.

* Anderson, Bernhard W., *Understanding the Old Testament.* Englewood Cliffs, N. J.: Prentice-Hall, Inc., 1957. A competent survey of the literature of Old Testament faith in its historical setting.

* Bewer, Julius A., *The Literature of the Old Testament,* 3rd. ed. Revised by Emil G. Kraeling. New York: Columbia University Press, 1962. A classic in its field, this book has been brought into contact with recent scholarship by its reviser.

* Bright, John, *A History of Israel*. Philadelphia: Westminster Press, 1959. A thorough study drawing heavily on interpretation of archaeological work.

———, *The Kingdom of God*. Nashville, Tenn.: Abingdon Press, 1953. Studies God's rule as understood in Old and New Testaments.

* Buber, Martin, *The Prophetic Faith*. Translated by Carlyle Witton-Davies. New York: Harper Torchbooks, 1960. Penetrating insight, through the eyes of a great Jewish scholar, into the faith of Israel as recorded in the Old Testament.

Eichrodt, Walther, *Theology of the Old Testament*, Vol. I. Translated by J. A. Baker. Philadelphia: Westminster Press, 1961. A theology concentrating on the meaning of "covenant."

Finegan, Jack, *Light from the Ancient Past: The Archaelogical Background of the Hebrew-Christian Religion*. Princeton: Princeton University Press, 1946. A fascinating description of the remains of ancient civilizations that illustrate the history and religion of the Old and New Testaments.

* Gottwald, Norman K., *A Light to the Nations*. New York: Harper & Row, Publishers, 1959. An introduction to the Old Testament placing Old Testament literature in its historical setting and emphasizing the perspective of faith from which the history was remembered and the literature composed.

Mowinckel, Sigmund, *He that Cometh*. Translated by G. W. Anderson. Nashville, Tenn.: Abingdon Press, 1954. A thorough study of the Messiah and related figures in the Old Testament and Judaism, which reflects the important contributions made in Old Testament study by Scandinavian scholars.

Napier, B. Davie, *From Faith to Faith*. New York: Harper & Row, Publishers, 1955. The theological unity of the Old Testament is stressed in this book.

———, *Song of the Vineyard*. New York: Harper & Row, Publishers, 1962. A "theological introduction to the Old Testament," written in the form of a "companion," that is, commenting on passages indicated in the margin.

Noth, Martin, *The History of Israel*, 2nd. ed. London: Adam & Charles Black, Ltd., 1960. In contrast to Bright, Noth holds that analysis of the literary sources rather than archaeology must be our principal key to the early history of the Hebrews.

Rad, Gerhard von, *Old Testament Theology*. New York: Harper & Row, Publishers, 1962. This work relates the theology of the Old

Testament to the study of the cultic and literary forms in which the tradition was preserved.

Rowley, H. H., ed., *The Old Testament and Modern Study*. Oxford: Clarendon Press, 1951. An important collection of essays on the Old Testament reflecting trends in scholarship up to 1950.

Wright, G. Ernest, *God Who Acts*. Naperville, Ill.: Alec E. Allenson, Inc., 1952. A presentation of biblical theology as recital or proclamation of the acts of God.

* ———— and Reginald H. Fuller, *The Book of the Acts of God*. New York: Doubleday Anchor Books, 1960. One of the most successful introductory books in bringing out the ways in which the Bible intends to confront its hearers. Covers Old and New Testaments.

V. The Intertestamental Period

Barrett, C. K., *The New Testament Background: Selected Documents*. New York: The Macmillan Co., 1957. A comprehensive collection of ancient writings, Jewish and pagan, which illustrate the background of the New Testament.

Gaster, Theodor H., ed., *The Dead Sea Scriptures in English Translation*. New York: Doubleday & Co., 1956. Of the many books on the Dead Sea or Qumran discoveries, only this one is listed as providing the most available translation of the documents themselves.

Pfeiffer, Robert H., *History of New Testament Times with an Introduction to the Apocrypha*. New York: Harper & Row, Publishers, 1949. A useful sketch of the historical background of the New Testament, with a discussion of the apocryphal books.

VI. New Testament History and Faith

* Bornkamm, Günther, *Jesus of Nazareth*. Translated by Irene and Fraser McLuskey with James M. Robinson. New York: Harper & Row, Publishers, 1960. Written out of the contemporary scholarly discussion, this book joins scholarly rigor with concern to set forth the faith of the gospels.

Bultmann, Rudolf, *Theology of the New Testament*. Translated by Kendrick Grobel. Two Volumes. New York: Charles Scribner's

Sons, 1951-55. Reflects Bultmann's existentialist interpretation of the New Testament. Particularly thorough on Paul and John.

Cullmann, Oscar, *Christ and Time*. Translated by Floyd V. Filson. Philadelphia: Westminster Press, 1950. An interpretation of the New Testament in terms of "redemptive history."

Hunter, Archibald M., *Interpreting Paul's Gospel*. Philadelphia: Westminster Press, 1954. An interpretation of the message of Paul.

* Kee, Howard Clark, and Franklin W. Young, *Understanding the New Testament*. Englewood Cliffs, N. J.: Prentice-Hall, Inc., 1957. A competent study of the New Testament, with emphasis on historical development.

Knox, John, *The Death of Christ*. Nashville, Tenn. Abingdon Press, 1958. A study of the Cross and the paradox of sacrifice and victory.

———, *Jesus: Lord and Christ*. New York: Harper & Row, Publishers, 1958. Gathers into one volume three works focusing on the life of Jesus, the memory and message of the early church, and the meaning of Christ to the church.

* Price, James L., *Interpreting the New Testament*. New York: Holt, Rinehart & Winston, Inc., 1961. A thorough and up-to-date study of the New Testament.

Richardson, Alan, *An Introduction to the Theology of the New Testament*. London: Student Christian Movement Press, 1958. A view of New Testament faith as a revolutionary reinterpretation of the Old Testament scheme of salvation.

Wilder, Amos N., *New Testament Faith for Today*. New York: Harper & Row, Publishers, 1955. A penetrating discussion of the New Testament in relation to our time.

* Wright, G. Ernest, and Reginald H. Fuller, *The Book of the Acts of God*. New York: Doubleday Anchor Books, 1960. One of the most successful introductory books in bringing out the ways in which biblical faith intends to confront its hearers. Covers Old and New Testaments.

VII. Reference Works

The Bible Today. London: The London Times, 1959. Essays on a wide variety of topics.

* Buttrick, George A., et al., eds., *The Interpreter's Bible*. Twelve Volumes. Nashville, Tenn.; Abingdon Press, 1951-57. Of great

usefulness. The general articles in Volumes I and VII are particularly helpful.

————, *The Interpreter's Dictionary of the Bible.* Four Volumes. Nashville, Tenn.: Abingdon Press, 1962. An excellent, thorough reference work.

Eiselen, Frederick C., et al., eds., *The Abingdon Bible Commentary.* Nashville, Tenn.: Abingdon Press, 1929. A useful one-volume commentary.

Hastings, James H., ed., *Dictionary of the Bible.* Revised ed. by F. C. Grant and H. H. Rowley. New York: Charles Scribner's Sons, 1963. Very thorough for a one-volume dictionary; emphasizes theological interpretation as well as historical data.

Manson, Thomas E., ed., *A Companion to the Bible.* New York: Charles Scribner's Sons, 1939. A collection of essays about the Bible. A very useful "companion" for the Bible student.

May, Herbert G., ed., *Oxford Bible Atlas.* New York: Oxford University Press, 1962. An excellent compact atlas.

Miller, Madeleine S. and J. Lane Miller, *Harper's Bible Dictionary.* New York: Harper & Row, Publishers, 1952. Particularly complete in its coverage of geographical and archaeological matters.

Richardson, Alan, ed., *A Theological Word Book of the Bible.* New York: The Macmillan Co., 1951. A dictionary that limits itself to the religious language of the Bible.

* Wright, G. Ernest and Floyd V. Filson, *The Westminster Historical Atlas to the Bible,* rev. ed. Philadelphia: Westminster Press, 1956. First-rate maps and an excellent brief sketch of Old and New Testament history.

Index of
Biblical Books

For books which are discussed in detail, the first reference indicates the principal discussion of the book. A list of the Apocrypha will be found on pages 173-174.

Old Testament

New Testament